CALL TO ACTION
OR
CALL TO APOSTASY?

How Dissenters Plan to Remake the Catholic Church in Their Own Image

by
Brian Clowes, PhD

Human Life International
Front Royal, Virginia
1997

© 1997 Human Life International

Human Life International
4 Family Life
Front Royal, VA 22630
(540) 635-7884
Fax: (540) 636-7363
E-mail: hli@hli.org
World Wide Web: http://www.hli.org

ISBN 1-55922-046-5

Printed in the United States of America.

For additional copies of this booklet, call HLI toll free at
(800) 549-LIFE

*This work is dedicated
to all of those
religious men and women
who remain faithful
to their vows.*

*All Scripture quotations are from the
Revised Standard Version of the Holy Bible.*

TABLE OF CONTENTS

V. Assault on the "Apostolic" Church

VI. Tactics of the Dissenters and How to Defeat Them

VII. How to Get Rid of the Dissenters
in Your Parish and Diocese

VIII. Summary and Conclusions

I. INTRODUCTION

*"I appeal to you, brethren, to take note of those who create
dissensions and difficulties, in opposition to the doctrine which you
have been taught; avoid them. For such persons do not serve our
Lord Christ, but their own appetites, and by fair and flattering words
they deceive the hearts of the simple-minded."*
~St. Paul's Letter to the Romans, 16:17-18

Subverting the Four Marks
of the Church

The great Chinese military strategist Sun Tzu wrote more
than 25 centuries ago in his classic *The Art of War,* "All
warfare is based primarily on the deception of an enemy.
Fighting on a battlefield is the most primitive way of making
war. There is no art higher than to destroy your enemy without a
fight—by subverting anything of value in your enemy's country."

Sun never imagined that, as we approach the Third Millennium, his strategies would be used to undermine and destroy the
very identity of the Roman Catholic Church.

The dissenters' primary objective is to undermine the four
marks of the Church, the marks by which we can unerringly
identify a church that is truly Roman Catholic. According to the
Catechism of the Catholic Church [#811], "These four character-
istics—one, holy, catholic and apostolic—inseparably linked
with each other, indicate essential features of the Church and her
mission."

If the dissenters can succeed in subverting and thus destroying the four marks of the Church, then they have re-molded Her
in their own image—a "church" that is not of God, but of man.

1

The dissenters may have done all of the physical work, but the humanist construct that will result has as its author none other than *Satan himself.*

Heresy, Apostasy and Schism

Indeed all who desire to live a godly life in Christ Jesus will be persecuted, while evil men and impostors will go on from bad to worse, deceivers and deceived. . . . For the time is coming when people will not endure sound teaching, but having itching ears they will accumulate for themselves teachers to suit their own likings, and will turn away from listening to the truth and wander into myths.
~2 Timothy 3:12-13, 4:3-4

The *Catechism* [#2089] distinguishes between heresy, apostasy and schism as follows: "Heresy is the obstinate post-baptismal denial of some truth which must be believed with divine and catholic faith, or it is likewise an obstinate doubt concerning the same; apostasy is the total repudiation of the Christian faith; schism is the refusal of submission to the Roman Pontiff or of communion with the members of the Church subject to him."

Dissenters stridently insist that they are not "heretics." They claim that the Catholic Church holds conscience to be the supreme arbiter of all decisions and, as long as a person acts "in accordance with his conscience," he is operating in the best of Catholic traditions. The dissenter's "conscience," of course, is a very flexible entity and, as we will see, excuses and rationalizes acts not only condemned by the Church, but by Jesus Christ Himself.

This booklet will show that Call to Action members and other dissenters are heretics in that they reject necessary Catholic truths. It will also show that the organized dissenters go far beyond "mere" heresy to complete apostasy, since their version of "Catholicism" is not only un-Catholic, it does not even slightly resemble anything Christian. The dissenters may also rightly be termed "schismatics," since they obstinately refuse to submit to the authority of the Roman Pontiff or the Magisterium, the teaching authority of the Roman Catholic Church, and instead hold as the supreme authority "conscience" and "personal experience."

The Purpose of This Work

Orthodox Catholics feel helplessness and anxiety as they see what dissenters are doing to Holy Mother Church, and the almost universal indifference that meets them. This leads to a kind of paralysis and an unwillingness to take action against heresy.

A feeling of helplessness is caused by a lack of power, and a lack of power is caused by disorganization. Anxiety is caused by uncertainty, and uncertainty is caused by lack of knowledge.

The purpose of this work is to give concerned orthodox Catholics basic information on the theory of dissent and dissenters, and some practical information on how to organize against them.

Before we can defeat Call to Action and its agenda, we must look upon ourselves as members of the Church Militant who have enlisted as Soldiers of Christ. Next, we need to study the dissenters in order to learn exactly what kind of people we are dealing with and what their beliefs are. Then we must delve into their tactics and learn how to thwart them. Finally, we must take concerted and organized action against them, while realizing that it is Satan, not the dissenters themselves, who is the real enemy.

This short work outlines these steps and seeks to encourage orthodox Catholics to step boldly onto the eternal battlefield in order to further the Culture of Life and defend the Church from Her many enemies.

II. ASSAULT ON THE "ONE" CHURCH

"But false prophets also arose among the people, just as there will be false teachers among you, who will secretly bring in destructive heresies, even denying the Master who bought them, bringing upon themselves swift destruction. And many will follow their licentiousness, and because of them the way of truth will be reviled. And in their greed they will exploit you with false words . . . They have eyes full of adultery, insatiable for sin. They entice unsteady souls. They have hearts trained in greed. Accursed children! Forsaking the right way they have gone astray; they have followed the way of Balaam, the son of Be'or, who loved gain from wrongdoing. . . . For, uttering loud boasts of folly, they entice with licentious passions of the flesh men who have barely escaped from those who live in error. They promise them freedom, but they themselves are slaves of corruption; for whatever overcomes a man, to that he is enslaved. . . . For it would have been better for them never to have known the way of righteousness than after knowing it to turn back from the holy commandment delivered to them. It has happened to them according to the true proverb, The dog turns back to his own vomit, and the sow is washed only to wallow in the mire."
~2 Peter 2:1-3, 14-15, 18-19, 21-22

What It Means to Be "One"

The essence of the Roman Catholic Church is the unity She derives from Her bridegroom, Christ. The worst wound to the unity of the Church is the separation of people from the Church through dissension and sin. The *Catechism* [#817] tells us that "Where there are sins, there are also divisions, schisms, heresies, and disputes. Where there is virtue, however, there also are harmony and unity, from which arise the one heart and one soul of all believers."

5

This contrast is vividly illustrated by professional dissenters such as those in Call to Action (CTA), who embrace and even *celebrate* such mortal sins as contraception, sterilization, masturbation, abortion, sodomy and divorce. As the dissenters strive for more and more open acceptance of what was formerly agreed to be sinful, the unity of the Church becomes more and more splintered. They speak of an endless array of stunted imitation "churches" such as AmChurch, HouseChurch, GreenChurch, FemChurch, NewChurch, WomenChurch, FutureChurch, FreeChurch, WeChurch and MeChurch—anything and everything but the authentic Roman Catholic Church.

Ultimately, as they implement concepts such as "small faith communities" and "constitutions" at every level, the dissenters hope that the Church will be reduced from a single immovable rock to a disorganized heap of pebbles, each of which is completely different from every other.

Institutionalizing Dissent Through "Constitutional" Action

Introduction

The Association for the Rights of Catholics in the Church (ARCC) was founded in 1980 in reaction to Vatican censure of such radical theologians as Edward Schillebeeckx, Jacques Pohier, and Hans Küng. The primary objective of ARCC is to agitate for shared decision-making between the clergy and the laity through the implementation of a "Constitution for the Catholic Church."

Hans Küng

ARCC's suggested "Constitution" closely parallels its "Charter of the Rights of Catholics in the Church," which itself is modeled not on Scripture, revelation or sacred tradition, but on the Charter of the United Nations. Fundamental to ARCC's "Constitution" and its "Charter" is a belief that all Catholics are "radically equal," whether they be ordained or laity, dissenting or faithful, living in a state of grace or wallowing in mortal sin. The "Charter" was signed by Call to Action and many other members of Catholic Organizations for Renewal, and all dissenting groups support all of its articles.

Many of the articles of ARCC's Charter seem reasonable to most uninformed Catholics, but their implementation would without question lead to total anarchy within the Church and the loss of millions of souls.

The Articles

All of the articles of ARCC's Constitution and Charter emphasize personal autonomy, freedom and conscience—not personal sanctification and sacrifice. This reduces ARCC's documents to nothing more than a mere list of demands.

The following paragraphs discuss the most important articles of the Charter.

Article #1: "All Catholics have the right to follow their informed consciences in all matters."

"... they disdain all authority and brook no restraint; and relying upon a false conscience, they attempt to ascribe to a love of truth that which is in reality the result of pride and obstinacy."
~Pope St. Pius X
Encyclical *Pascendi Dominici Gregis*
("On the Doctrine of the Modernists")
September 8, 1907, #3

The first article of ARCC's "Charter" is the most important of all. Dissenters passionately believe that the final arbiter of any decision must be the person's conscience, regardless of whether it is properly formed or not. Of course, if the Church accepts this "ideal," the original standard—reliance on an informed conscience *based on the authority of the Magisterium*—will be swept away, to be replaced by a mandate for pure moral relativism.

Anthony Padovano, co-founder and President of CORPUS, the National Society for a Married Priesthood, concluded his talk at the 1996 CTA National Convention by frankly advocating the replacement of the Holy Catholic Church with a humanistic construct: "When the cathedral is destroyed, a new temple of *conscience and the spirit* is built by more than human hands. . . . our fundamental question in the Church should not be about whether something is Catholic, but whether it is healthy and holy and *human*, for if it is all of these, then it is Catholic also."[1]

Those who embrace the supremacy of human conscience *by definition* discard objective truth, because the unfettered "conscience" is notoriously flexible, compromising and rationalizing when temptation strikes. Just as importantly, since a person whose conscience reigns supreme will inevitably fall into sin and then *accept* that sin, he will also be more tolerant of sin in others. Another co-founder of CORPUS, Frank Bonnike, says that "I keep all the rules, but I also respect people who don't keep all the rules. The key is to respect their conscience."[2]

Dissenters are very fond of quoting the Vatican II document *Dignitatis Humanae* ("Declaration on Religious Freedom"), in support of their contention that we should be able to do anything our "conscience" does not object to.

However, Father John Courtney Murray, S.J., principal author of the *Declaration*, anticipated this kind of dishonesty. He stated in a footnote to the Abbott-Gallagher edition of the Council texts that:

> The *Declaration* does not base the right to the free exercise of religion on "freedom of conscience." Nowhere does this phrase occur. And the *Declaration* nowhere lends its authority to the theory for which the phrase frequently stands, namely, that I have the right to do what my conscience tells me to do, simply because my conscience tells me to do it. This is a perilous theory. Its particular peril is subjectivism— the notion that, in the end, it is my conscience, and not the objective truth, which determines what is right and wrong, true or false.[3]

8

The dissenters also conveniently neglect to mention paragraph 8 of the *Declaration*, which notes that ". . . not a few can be found who seem inclined to use the name of freedom as the pretext for refusing to submit to authority and for making light of the duty of obedience."

The correct connection between freedom and truth as it *should* be perceived by the conscience, and the role of the Magisterium, is outlined by Pope John Paul II in his encyclical *Veritatis Splendor* ("The Splendor of Truth"), #61-64:

> Consequently "in the practical judgment of conscience," which imposes on the person the obligation to perform a given act, "the link between freedom and truth is made manifest." Precisely for this reason conscience expresses itself in acts of "judgment" which reflect the truth about the good, and not in arbitrary "decisions." The maturity and responsibility of these judgments—and, when all is said and done, of the individual who is their subject—are not measured by the liberation of the conscience from objective truth, in favor of an alleged autonomy in personal decisions, but, on the contrary, by an insistent search for truth and by allowing oneself to be guided by that truth in one's actions.
>
> Christians have a great help for the formation of conscience "in the Church and her Magisterium." As the Council affirms: "In forming their consciences the Christian faithful must give careful attention to the sacred and certain teaching of the Church. For the Catholic Church is by the will of Christ the teacher of truth. Her charge is to announce and teach authentically that truth which is Christ, and at the same time with her authority to declare and confirm the principles of the moral order which derive from human nature itself." It follows that the authority of the Church, when she pronounces on moral questions, in no way undermines the freedom of conscience of Christians.

We can say with some authority that the dissenters don't *really* believe that "All Catholics have the right to follow their informed consciences in all matters," because, when orthodox Catholics "follow their consciences" and oppose abortion, homosexual "marriage" and contraception, groups like ARCC stridently condemn them and ridicule their views. As with "tolerance" and "nonjudgmentalism," the glorification of "conscience" is a mere smoke screen that dissenters use to further their goals.

Article #2: "Officers of the Church have the right to teach on matters both of private and public morality only after wide consultation with the faithful prior to the formulation of the teaching."

This is also a very important article in ARCC's Constitution, and highlights the primary defect in the "Catholic Common Ground Project" (CCGP).

If a group of people with diverse backgrounds meets to discuss the morality of a particular act, and if one of the ground rules of the discussion is "tolerance for the viewpoints of others," the inevitable result will be the "lowest common denominator"—only that position that is most tolerant and nonjudgmental, or, in other words, most liberal.

This, of course, is exactly what the dissenters want—a "democratic" system of consultation that *guarantees* that their objectives will be "voted in" by the people through their version of "dialogue," as described in Section V.

More fundamentally, Article #2 of the Constitution completely rejects objective truth by subjecting moral decisions to a public vote.

Article #5: "All Catholics have the right to a voice in all decisions that affect them, including the choosing of their leaders."

Under the regime envisioned by Article #5, authority is not conferred by God through Holy Orders, but from the will and the vote of the people. The Women's Ordination Conference (WOC) and other dissenting groups agree that priests should be replaced by "community-ordained facilitators" or "practitioners" who are given their position by the authority of the people in the parish.[4]

A priest does not offer the Sacrifice of the Mass or confer any other Sacrament by the consent of the people, but by the authority of Christ. To change this means that the Sacraments are not *of* Christ; therefore, they lose all their power to sanctify. The Sacraments become mere rituals of the type commonly practiced at Call to Action conferences, where lay people speak the words of consecration.

The dissenters know very well that, if women are "ordained" under their system, they would all be extremely liberal, since orthodox Catholic women would automatically exclude themselves from the process. The result would be a flood of untrained "priestesses" who would enthusiastically promote abortion and homosexuality, and who would relentlessly condemn the remnants of the "patriarchal" church from the pulpit. This is an experience being suffered by the Episcopal Church right now, and thinking Catholics should note the sad consequences suffered by other churches that have ordained women.

Article #8: "All Catholics have the right to express publicly their dissent in regard to decisions made by Church authorities."

Modernist organizations justify their actions by claiming that their dissent is "for the good of the Church." The dissenting organization Celibacy Is The Issue (CITI) shows that dissenters actually pursue institutionalized Humanism and situation ethics:

> Catholic Christianity is a living faith, not a dead imitation of a past which no longer exists. Catholic theology is a contemporary reflection in today's thought categories on present questions and problems about what it means to think and live as a Catholic Christian in this concrete world. To parrot the past is to pervert it. To be a Christian means to make what Jesus thought, taught and wrought understandable and applicable in today's language and life. Christian life and theology must be something dynamic, not dead, and therefore at its heart there must be deliberation, dissent, dialogue, decision. . . .[5]

Veritatis Splendor [#4] shows us that systematic and widespread dissent actually disconnects human freedom from truth, thus blinding people to the distinction between *licit* and *illicit* freedoms:

> [A] new situation has come about *within the Christian community itself*, which has experienced the spread of numerous doubts and objections of a human and psychological, social and cultural, religious and even properly theological nature, with regard to the Church's moral teachings. It is no longer a matter of limited and occasional dissent, but of an overall and systematic calling into question of traditional moral doctrine, on the basis of certain anthropological and ethical presuppositions. At the root of these presuppositions is the more or less obvious influence of currents of thought which end by detaching human freedom from its essential and constitutive relationship to truth.

When justifying systematic dissent, liberal Catholics speak constantly of Vatican II, and occasionally justify their actions with *Lumen Gentium* [#37]: "By reason of the knowledge, competence or pre-eminence which they have, the laity are empowered—indeed sometimes obliged— to manifest their opinion on those things which pertain to the good of the Church." However, liberal Catholics ignore the passage that immediately follows: "Like all Christians, the laity should promptly accept in Christian obedience what is decided by the pastors who, as teachers and rulers of the Church, represent Christ." Even more telling is *Lumen Gentium* [#20], which proclaims: ". . . The bishops have by divine institution taken the place of the apostles as pastors of the Church, in such wise that whoever listens to them is listening to Christ and whoever despises them despises Christ and him who sent Christ."[6]

If a person cannot distinguish between licit and illicit freedoms, he becomes lost in the featureless landscape of moral relativism, and there is no hope that he can discern the objective truth in any situation. This is one of the most effective tactics used by Satan to ensnare souls.

The great paradox of situational ethics lies in the fact that, when its practitioners gain power, they ruthlessly stifle dissent to *their* opinions and regulations. This has been proven by Call to Action itself, which, at its inauguration in Detroit in 1976, systematically suppressed and ridiculed orthodox Catholic speakers. This has also been demonstrated at the last several United Nations conferences, where organized feminists attempted to enshrine abortion as a "basic human right" while suppressing all opposing voices.

The CTA-type "New Age" liberal claims that he or she will "fight to the death for your right to free speech," while simultaneously drawing up a long list of exceptions. They say that orthodox Catholics may not assemble outside abortion mills because this causes a "climate of fear and violence"; may not speak out against the homosexual agenda because this creates "an atmosphere of homophobia;" and may not oppose women's ordination, because this is "misogynist." In other words, orthodox Catholics may say anything they want to say—as long as liberals approve of the message.

Article #9: "All Catholics have the right to be dealt with according to commonly accepted norms of fair administrative and judicial procedures without undue delay."

Under the complicated system formulated under ARCC's "Constitution," it would literally be impossible to impose any sanctions on any person for any violation of any rule, no matter how flagrant—unless, of course, they were orthodox, in which case the system would work very efficiently indeed. This is because the "Constitution" and "Charter" would construct a tribunal bureaucracy of such extraordinary complexity and with so many layers of authority that it would be impossible to prosecute even the most egregious violation of Church law. Since this bureaucracy would be staffed by liberals, selective enforcement of the law would be the norm. The entire structure would be even more difficult to navigate than the United States court system.

Of course, if the Catholic Church became Americanized, any orthodox remnant could be prosecuted with impunity under this system, and orthodox Catholics could expect no recourse, similar to the situation experienced by pro-life rescuers and picketers in countries where a liberal court system is in place.

Article #15: "All Catholics, regardless of race, age, nationality, sex, sexual orientation, state-of-life, or social position have the right to receive all the sacraments for which they are adequately prepared."

This means that anyone, even if they are in a state of mortal sin, may receive the Sacraments of Communion, Confirmation, Holy Orders, and Matrimony, thus committing the sin of sacrilege. As described in Section III, dissenters think that they have absolutely no use for the Sacrament of Confession, since they have neatly defined "sin" as something that *others* commit.

Article #16: "All Catholics, regardless of canonical status (lay or clerical), sex or sexual orientation, have the right to exercise all ministries in the Church for which they are adequately prepared, according to the needs and with the approval of the community."

This call for women's ordination is repeated in Article #26 of ARCC's "Charter," which states that "All Catholic women have an equal right with men to the resources and the exercise of all the powers of the Church."

Article #20: "Catholic teachers of theology have a right to responsible academic freedom. The acceptability of their teaching is to be judged in dialogue with their peers, keeping in mind the legitimacy of responsible dissent and pluralism of belief."

In other words, all belief systems will be treated as equal, and situational ethics will be enshrined as the principle under which Catholic universities and high schools will operate—not an authentic search for the truth.

Article #28: "All married Catholics have the right to determine in conscience the size of their families and the appropriate methods of family planning."

Pro-life activists know that "family planning" is a pro-abortion weasel-word meaning a total acceptance of abortion, sterilization, and all means of contraceptive and abortifacient birth control.

Articles #30 and #31: "All married Catholics have the right to withdraw from a marriage which has irretrievably broken down. All such Catholics retain the radical right to remarry. . . . All Catholics who are divorced and remarried and who are in conscience reconciled to the Church have the right to the same ministries, including all sacraments, as do other Catholics."

Dissenters will often go to extraordinary lengths to rationalize the sins that they commit. In the case of divorce, Mary Grace Crowley-Kock of CORPUS goes so far as to ask, "The question is: What would Jesus do in these circumstances? Would Jesus say, 'I'm sorry, a man-made church law does not allow you to get married because you didn't get an annulment,' or would he say, 'Here are two people who are in love, who ask that their marriage be blessed and who are inviting Jesus to be in their midst.' I can't imagine Jesus coming across and saying that this is wrong."[7]

What Crowley-Kock "can't imagine" actually *did* occur, and the Apostles Matthew [19:9], Mark [10:11-12] and Luke [16:18] all recorded Our Lord proclaiming "Whoever divorces his wife and marries another, commits adultery against her; and if she divorces her husband and marries another, she commits adultery."

If dissenters can ignore such a direct statement made by Our Lord Himself in no less an authoritative text than the *Gospels*, we know their ability to deceive themselves knows no boundaries.

15

Article #32: "All Catholics have the right to expect that Church documents and materials will avoid sexist language, and that symbols and imagery of God will not be exclusively masculine."

Yet again, the dissenters are trying to rewrite Church history and even Scripture. Our Lord did *not* say, "Our Father/Mother Who art in Heaven" [Mt 6:9]. He did *not* say, "Whosoever acknowledges Me before men, I will acknowledge before My Mother in Heaven" [Mt 10:32]. And He certainly did *not* say, "For the Son of man shall come in the glory of his Father and/or Mother with his angels . . ." [Mt 16:27]. Even though Jesus refers to God as "Father" well over a hundred times in the Gospels, the dissenters' mad zeal for change still drives them to attempt to expunge the "maleness" of God from the Bible.

Enacting the "Constitution"

ARCC's "Constitution for the Catholic Church," which mirrors the "Charter" described above, would be enacted by a Constitutional Convention named Vatican III. This would undoubtedly be a convention heavily loaded with liberals who would ruthlessly stifle and ridicule traditional and orthodox voices—just as happened at the original 1976 Detroit conference where Call to Action was founded.

In addition to the worldwide "Constitution," ARCC urges that every continent, nation, diocese and parish have its own detailed Constitution, whose articles and amendments would be arrived at by popular vote of the bodies of individuals concerned. A lower level would not be subordinate in any way to a higher level, and so these "concentric circles" ["Constitution," article IIIB3c], would lead to a riot of conflicting rules that would completely paralyze any attempt by Rome to impose order, thereby fulfilling the dissenters' dream of "the destruction of the hierarchical church."

For just one moment, try to imagine what society would be like if every block, town, county and state were allowed to make up its own laws and rules without interference from any higher authority. White supremacists could fulfill their dreams of a homeland in the Northwest, where Blacks could be expelled or enslaved. Radical Black Muslims could eject Jews from their neighborhoods. Homosexuals could be expelled from areas where they were not welcome. Laws would be completely different from city to city and county to county, and absolute anarchy would reign.

Interestingly, one of the most effective arguments used by liberals in the past to support their demands was a condemnation of a "patchwork quilt of laws," which forced people to check the ordinances of every jurisdiction so that they could be sure they were not in violation. Yet the liberals support just such a "crazy quilt" within the Catholic Church, since they know that such a situation would create uncontrollable anarchy, where all varieties of heresy and sin could flourish and be accepted publicly.

Such a system of constitutional "concentric circles" would also create an impenetrable bureaucracy without equal. Every jurisdiction would be overseen by co-chairs, a "clergyperson" and a lay person. At the highest level would be a "General Council," co-chaired by the Pope and a lay person, that would "function as the main decision-making body of the universal Church" and would "set policy concerning doctrine, morals, worship . . ." [IIICe13 and 16].

This system would render Church operation so incredibly complex that literally any activity could be justified or defended for years in the confusion. So many layers of "rights" would exist that no flagrant dissent could ever be prosecuted, thereby permanently institutionalizing confusion and disorientation of the laity. This would be a huge step towards the ultimate goal of the dissenters, which is unlimited personal freedom without guilt.

Under the ARCC system, the American Catholic Church would closely resemble the United States government, but would not be as disciplined or as logically organized. Parish councils would elect pastors from among the people for one non-renewable five-year term. Bishops would be elected for ten-year terms by delegates from the "National Council," in a process similar to primary elections. Finally, the Pope would be elected by a convention of "National Councils" [IIICa2].

Section IV of the "Constitution" would set up a very complicated judicial system that would in practice guarantee that
nobody would ever be punished, regardless of the degree of their
offense. There would be diocesan, national and international
tribunals, culminating in a Supreme Tribunal whose job would
be to "hear cases charging illegal or unconstitutional actions by
the Pope." Under the "Constitution," of course, such violations
could include the Pope taking action against dissenters, promul-
gating authentic dogma or teaching on any subject without wide
consultation with the people, or even canonizing Saints who did
not champion liberal causes.

Section IVBc3 of the "Constitution" warns darkly that "There
shall be no judicial appeal from the judgments of the Supreme
Tribunal."

Changing the Rules to Encourage and Enable Dissent

"Beware lest any man spoil you through philosophy and vain deceit,
after the tradition of men, after the rudiments of the world,
and not after Christ."
~Colossians 2:8

There are millions of voluntary, non-democratic associations in existence all over the world today, including
corporations, armed forces, sports teams and fraternal
organizations. The members of these organizations unite for a
common purpose and, for this reason, agree to conduct themselves in a manner suited to achieving their purpose. If the
members of the association want to compete and succeed against
other groups in their class, they must frequently place the good
of the organization above their own individual interests. When
they do this, all members of the group benefit.

The Roman Catholic Church is no different from secular
associations in this respect. The Church is a voluntary, non-
democratic association of individuals united for a common
purpose—in this case, to compete for souls against the Culture

of Death. The mission of true Catholics is to know, love and serve God and assist others in achieving sanctity.

Dissenters would like to destroy or disable everything in the Church that sanctifies Catholics, including the Sacraments, the teaching of objective truth, and the hierarchy. They claim that many evils spring from a hierarchical organization, but they never complain about identical "problems" that are features of sports teams, the military, corporations or legal firms.

Imagine what would happen if a person declared his desire to join a basketball team, and then told the coach that he refused to wear the uniform because it detracted from his individuality; that he could not dribble well, and so demanded the right to carry the ball; that he was too out of shape to jump, and so the basket should be lowered a couple of feet. Such a person would be laughed off the court!

All voluntary organizations are led by a chief executive officer (CEO), senior partner, general, admiral or coach.

All such groups have rules that every member must follow if the organization is to succeed in its mission and to avoid descending into anarchy. And every member has a right to leave the organization at any time, if not bound by a contract.

The "Star Trek" Example

The arguments used by the dissenters to buttress their "case" against the hierarchy are often laughable. For example, Linda Pinto of CORPUS, a former Franciscan nun now married to a former diocesan priest, says that:

> Thirty years ago this past month a series called "Star Trek" was aired on TV. Its premise was that all celestial people, human and otherwise, could live together in genuine community. Their diversity would be affirmed, celebrated and respected, and the strength that resulted would unify them into one. Gender, race, marital status, economics, ethnic background, would not qualify them for inclusion *or* exclusion in positions of power or service. Governance was collegial and consensual. Primacy of conscience was paramount. They call it their "Prime Directive." The current series on TV even

19

features a female captain— read Pope—who empowers, embraces and enables her crew by loving leadership. This sounds like good church to me.[8]

Linda Pinto of CORPUS

Apparently Pinto is as abysmally ignorant of "Star Trek" as she is of Church discipline, but her inept parallel serves to illustrate some basic principles. To begin with, governance is hardly "collegial and consensual" on a starship. The fictional "Star Fleet" is not a democratic institution any more than the Catholic Church is—in fact, it possesses a hierarchy that is so well-defined that anyone can distinguish the rank and position of a person merely by glancing at his or her collar. In the Church, as in Star Fleet, a hierarchy is absolutely essential to discipline, teaching and efficient operation.

Conscience is not paramount in Star Fleet, as Pinto alleges. Both Captain James Kirk and Mr. Spock risked "excommunication" from Star Fleet at various times and were disciplined for violating the "Prime Directive," which had nothing to do with conscience, but was instead a strict rule against interfering with the development of primitive cultures. In other words, following one's conscience is no more an excuse for violating dogma in Star Fleet than it is in the Catholic Church.

Why Don't the Dissenters Just *Leave?*

Dissenters offer many explanations as to why they want to stay in the Catholic Church, almost all of which are couched in impressibly altruistic language. For instance, Women-Church Convergence claims that "Safety is a human right. We strive to dismantle hierarchical structures and to end discrimination because they can result in insult and injury."[9]

The Modernists frequently cast themselves in the role of victims as they make absurd parallels between their own situations and those of genuine victims. Rosemary Ruether compares

20

Catholics to battered women as she tries to cover up the real reason she stays in the Church:

> "How can you stay in the Church?" some ask, much as an impatient social worker might ask a battered woman why she can't bring herself to leave her abusive husband. . . . The sin against the Holy Spirit is trying to evade that good news of God's gift of repentance by claiming that we have certainty and impeccability in our own hands—that we are Christ's church and so are preserved from serious error and corporate sin. This is where the church as an institution circles its wagons against the threat of grace, the threat of the Holy Spirit, the threat of repentance. We build our fortifications ever higher, claiming that anything we have taught a long time cannot be wrong. We justify our sins by their longevity.[10]

The author of this work polled participants in the 1996 Call to Action National Convention in Detroit, asking them, "Why do you stay in the Church?" The typical answer was "To heal the Church of its many sins." These "sins," of course, were racism, "homophobia," "sexism" and anti-Semitism—all corporate sins that require no self-examination or personal repentance other than an increased commitment to "tolerance" and "nonjudgmentalism."

What Call to Action desires is the classic shift of focus from personal to collective sin that has emasculated and destroyed so many mainline Protestant churches. CTA urges Church leaders to spend less energy, money and publicity on questions of sexual morality and more on social justice, combatting racism and ethnic discrimination, promoting peace and non-violence, and the environment. As if to highlight CTA's disinterest in personal sin, there was not one mention of confession (either scheduled or on-request) in the entire 30-page conference program for the 1996 National Convention. By contrast, the Call to Holiness conference, held at the same time just fifteen miles away, had at least two priests hearing confessions every day for several hours.

When the author asked CTA convention-goers the question "What motivates you?," they revealed the *true* reason that dissenters stay in the Church. They typically responded that

21

"The Church has absolutely no right to make us feel guilty about activities that our consciences tell us are moral."

This desperate desire to escape guilt permeates the dissenters' writings. Dianne Neu and Mary Hunt of the "Women's Alliance for Theology, Ethics and Ritual" (WATER), who are lesbian "life companions,"[4] claim that "Painful accusations are made against women who have abortions. Rather than seeing that women have the abortions they *need*, not the abortions they *want*, women who choose abortion are made to feel guilty and judged to be 'out of the church.'"[11]

As long as the Roman Catholic Church exists in Her current form, and as long as Her teachings on moral issues remain inviolate, Her very existence will be a rebuke to those committing immoral acts, and will cause them to feel guilty. So the dissenters' emphasis is not on personal repentance and sanctification, but the removal of the sensation of guilt while continuing and justifying their past and current behavior.

The only way dissenters can be free of this feeling of guilt is if everyone in society accepts their immoral acts. And the only way to achieve this is to drain the Church of Her vitality, in the same way a host of tiny spiders drains the vital fluids from a beautiful butterfly.

The "community" of dissent has become a sect of schismatics which has gradually burrowed into the structure of the Church like termites (almost two-thirds of CTA convention attendees work for the Church). Like termites, they feed off the structure of the Church. Unlike previous heretics, they do not have the honesty simply to *leave* the Church. They know that, if they leave, they will be nothing special. They will be just another gaggle of splinter groups in the great world supermarket of churches and false religions.

There is a more practical reason that dissenters stay in the Church. For most dissenters, to leave the Church would mean to give up their paychecks, because they are full-time workers in the Church. A majority of the people who attend Call to Action and Women's Ordination Conference (WOC) conventions, for instance, are pastoral assistants, teachers at Catholic schools and seminaries, or directors of religious education.[4]

22

On "Playing the Game"

If a person refuses to play by the rules of a game, he is almost always barred from playing that game. If a basketball player insists on travelling, he will eventually be ejected. If a card shark insists on cheating, he will be identified as a cheater and nobody will play with him. If a soldier refuses to salute, wear a uniform, or carry a rifle, he will be court-martialled and thrown out of the service.

The same holds true of the "games" of life and religion. If a person constantly preys on others, he is not playing by the rules that society has set down, and, if he persists in his predatory activities, he will eventually be separated from society or even "ejected" from life through capital punishment if his crimes are serious enough.

Every faithful Catholic has heard ignorant bigots sneer "if da Pope no play-a da game, he no make-a da rules," with regards to abortion and contraception. These people are missing the point. The Pope is not a *player* in the "game" of life; for orthodox Catholics, he is the *coach and referee*. And if so-called "members" of the team (members of the Catholic Church) do not play by the rules, then they should be "cut" from the team by excommunication. We might take the "play the game" remark and turn it around to use against the so-called "Catholic" abortophiles and other dissenters: "If you no play-a by de rules, you no play-a de game."

After all, what's fair is fair—*for everyone!*

One of the worst offenders in this area is Anthony Padovano, the current President of CORPUS (the National Society for a Married Priesthood), who claims that no person in the Church has the right to make rules unless he has *personal experience* in the area. He even declares that a faithful Catholic literally *cannot act with integrity or honesty:*

> I am suggesting that any other kind of Catholicism other than "conscience," or so-called "cafeteria" Catholicism, makes it highly unlikely that a believer can act with integrity, honesty and personal commitment. . . . "conscience" or so-called "cafeteria" Catholicism is infinitely more beneficial for the

Church than cathedral Catholicism. . . . Cathedral Catholicism does not give us a community of believers, but an assembly of servants and slaves. . . . Cathedral Catholicism will simply not be effective in the contemporary world when people are given no voice and when their lives and witness count for nothing, they do not believe. . . . Let me take as one example the approach to birth control. Cathedral Catholicism places the decision of its morality on just one person. This one person is not married, and almost all those consulted are *also* not married. The witness of married Catholics—sensitive, intelligent, committed Catholics—their witness over the years rejecting this teaching, and rejecting it in virtually unanimous numbers makes no difference.[1]

Padovano's heavy reliance on human experience as a guide for moral decision-making only confirms what Pope St. Pius X said in *Pascendi Dominici Gregis:* "For the Modernist believer, on the contrary, it is an established and certain fact that the reality of the divine does really exist in itself and quite independently of the person who believes in it. If you ask on what foundation this assertion of the believer rests, he answers: In the personal experience of the individual" [#14].

Dissenters commonly complain that "arbitrary decisions" about sexual matters such as priestly celibacy or birth control are made by "one person." They ignore the fact that such teachings have been taught *semper ubique omnes*—always, everywhere, and by everyone—and this fact makes them part of the ordinary and universal Magisterial teaching.[12]

If, of course, this Modernist/dissenter philosophy becomes ascendant, there will be as many religions as there are individuals, because everyone has different experiences during his or her lifetime. Once again, such a philosophy is antithetical to the "oneness" of the Roman Catholic Church, and to embrace it means that the body of the Church will be completely divided and therefore completely ineffectual in its mission of saving souls.

III. ASSAULT ON THE "HOLY" CHURCH

"[This is] the apologetic method of the Modernists, in perfect harmony with their doctrines—methods and doctrines replete with errors, made not for edification but for destruction, not for the making of Catholics but for the seduction of those who are Catholics into heresy; and tending to the utter subversion of all religion. . . . And now with Our eyes fixed upon the whole system, no one will be surprised that We should define it to be the synthesis of all heresies. . . . their system means the destruction not of the Catholic religion alone, but of all religion . . . by how many roads Modernism leads to atheism and to the annihilation of all religion."

~Pope St. Pius X
Encyclical *Pascendi Dominici Gregis*
("On the Doctrine of the Modernists")
September 8, 1907, #37, 39

What It Means to Be "Holy"

The *Catechism* [#824] states that "United with Christ, the Church is sanctified by him; through him and with him she becomes sanctifying. . . . All the activities of the Church are directed, as toward their end, to the sanctification of men in Christ and the glorification of God."

By stark contrast, the objective of the dissenters is the glorification of *themselves* through the new religion of Humanism. Dissenters are unfailingly *self-centered*. They prattle on endlessly about "*self*-fulfillment," "*self*-actualization," "*self*-affirmation," "*self*-esteem," always "*self*" and never "others." The only "selfs" they never speak of are *self*-control, *self*-discipline and *self*-sacrifice. They have given up theology for "*me*-ology."

One thing is certain: Self-centeredness eventually leads to cowardice. There are no martyrs among the dissenters.

The Saints have acknowledged that the first step to true holiness is acknowledgement of our own sinful natures [*Catechism*, #827].

There was absolutely no acknowledgement of personal sin during the 1996 CTA convention. Despite the fact that this gathering was attended by several bishops and more than 400 priests, there was not a single scheduled session of Confession, nor was Confession mentioned even once in any of the more than sixty talks, except occasionally in a derogatory or dismissive manner.

Ignoring Personal Sin to Dispel Guilt

Call to Action has followed the example of the world by emphasizing *communal* sin while downplaying *personal* sin. CTA speakers and "theologians" repeatedly emphasize that we are *all* guilty of the "sins" of racism, sexism, unjust income distribution, poverty, "eco-terrorism," "heterosexism/homo-hatred" and "all forms of violence, especially against women and children."

Article 4 of the "We Are Church" Referendum holds that "We believe in a church which affirms: the goodness of sexuality, the primacy of conscience in deciding issues of sexual morality (for example: birth control), the human rights of all persons regardless of sexual orientation, and the importance and urgency of issues other than sexual morality (for example: peace and non-violence, social justice, preservation of the environment)."

Dissenters often claim that they believe in a Church that "affirms the goodness of human sexuality." Translated, this *really* means "the more sex, regardless of type, the better." In reality, only faithful and orthodox Catholicism goes beyond affirmation and actually *safeguards* the goodness of human sexuality, which is so special that it can only be right for a man and a woman who have committed themselves to each other "until death do them part." CTAers instead embrace or tolerate everything that tends to cheapen and tarnish the sacredness of sex, and they reject both the procreative and unitive aspects of marriage by advocating fornication, masturbation, sodomy and other homosexual acts, divorce, contraception, sterilization and abortion.

This is how the Devil works: being a created creature, he cannot create anything himself, so he must twist God's gift of pure love between man and woman into a galaxy of perversions.

Dissenters would like to believe that we are *all* guilty of the same sins, because then nobody is really any better or different than anyone else, and the guilt that tortures them—the guilt that arises from the stark contrast between sin and sanctity—vanishes.

Dissenters will go to any lengths in order to rationalize their own sinful behavior. Their papers, books and speeches are saturated with misquotes, historical errors and outright deliberate deception through misrepresentation of the Church's historical teachings and of Scripture. Anthony Padovano shows the lengths to which the guilty will go to delude themselves when he says that "The forgiving father, in the parable [of the prodigal son], ignores the sexual charges, much as Jesus does with the woman in adultery. . . . And so, Jesus says little about sexuality and is gentle in dealing with sexual misconduct, not because he is unconcerned but precisely because he does not see this as our worst evil."[13]

Jesus certainly did *not* "ignore the sexual charges"—He instructed the adulterous woman to "go, and do not sin again" [John 8:4-11]. Padovano completely ignores the fact that Scripture—and especially the Gospels—condemns sexual sins more frequently than any other type of sin.[14]

How the Dissenters Distort History to Make a "Point"

Padovano is one of the worst offenders when it comes to distorting the history of the Church and slandering some of Her greatest pontiffs, all for the purpose of propping up insupportable arguments. For example, he has written that:

. . . As the century began, Pius X sought to destroy not lives as such but intelligence and learning in the Church. We became a ghetto against the world, belligerent and supposedly infallible, isolated and angry. Pius created a Catholic Gulag in which all who did not think and speak as one man did would be punished. This was the age of modernism and the penalties were severe: excommunication and denial of sacraments; destruction of careers, reputations, ministries; vilification and refusal of Catholic burial. A reign of terror was created and it sought its victims systematically and relentlessly. The whole world was allegedly wrong and only the infallible Pope was reliable. Thus, power, dominative and oppressive, narrow and self-righteous, cruel and sadistic was in place. . . . The reign of terror conducted by Pius X did not succeed. No reign of terror ever does.

John Paul II became even more harsh, almost obsessed on sexual issues. . . . he has gutted the Synod of Bishops, deni-grated episcopal conferences and defined the papacy in the code of Canon Law as accountable to God alone. Human rights in the Church exist only to the extent the Pope permits; Christian unity has fared badly; women at large do not find him their advocate. We know the story well.[13]

Padovano claims that Pope John Paul II is supposedly "obsessed on sexual issues." He ignores the fact that less than *five percent* of the writings and homilies of the current pontiff have addressed sexual matters.

The people who are really "hung up" on sex are the *dissenters*. A casual perusal of their literature reveals that between one-fourth and one-half of their writings deal with sex-related subjects such as contraception, abortion, priestly celibacy and homosexuality. This is necessary, because, in order to avoid their sad burden of guilt, the dissenters must continually labor to reassure each other that they are just as good as everyone else.

Anyone familiar with human nature knows that people who feel compelled to say this really don't believe it themselves.

Padovano demonstrates how dissenters will even pervert the teachings of the Early Church Fathers to make his points. He alleges that, "A rigid, cruel sexual ethic is now put in place. . . . it prompts Augustine to label 'sordid, filthy and horrible' a woman's embrace."[13]

28

Any reasonably competent student of St. Augustine, one of the first Fathers of the Church, knows that such a phrase is completely out of character for him. In point of fact, he *did* make this statement—but it was his unique style to paraphrase such heresies before refuting them. Augustine made the above statement as a summary of one of the principle beliefs of the Manichaeans—and then decisively refuted it—in his classic work *On the Morals of the Manichaeans.*[15]

Surrendering to the "New Age" Menace

"Here it is well to note at once that, given this doctrine of experience united with that of symbolism, every religion, even that of paganism, must be held to be true. . . . Modernists do not deny, but actually maintain, some confusedly, others frankly, that all religions are true."
~Pope St. Pius X
Encyclical *Pascendi Dominici Gregis*
("On the Doctrine of the Modernists")
September 8, 1907, #14

Square Pegs and Round Holes . . .

St. Augustine once remarked that there is a God-shaped hole in every person which only Jesus Christ can fill. Pity the poor dissenters. The "Jesus" they believe in is not authentic; to them, he is a mere prophet, no more divine than the rest of us. His principal and only perfections are tolerance and nonjudgmentalism, and he is perfectly willing to accept us just the way we are. The dissenters have fallen into a form of idolatry; the "god" they worship does not exist.

The dissenters are truly "children of a *looser* god." And, since this "god" of theirs only partially and imperfectly re-sembles the One True God, they desperately cast about for a "supplement" that will make them feel better about their nagging lack of spiritual fulfillment and vitality.

29

Satan Steps In

It has been said that Satan has many tools, but the lie is the handle that fits them all.

One of his most effective tools has an almost infinite variety of facets: the "New Age" religions, which have captured millions of souls for him. Dissenters forget that there are only two sources of supernatural power: Jesus Christ and Satan. Since the "New Age" is not of Christ, by a simple process of elimination, it must be of Satan.

Many dissenters have "evolved" to the point where their faith is no longer Catholic and no longer even Christian, but purely pagan. The "New Age" phenomenon is less a movement than a glittering rainbow of pantheistic and polytheistic practices with a flavor for every taste, no matter how esoteric.

In *Pascendi Dominici Gregis*, Pope St. Pius X recognized the two causes of Modernism as pride (as described in Section IV) and curiosity about things that are injurious to one's faith:

> To penetrate still deeper into the meaning of Modernism and to find a suitable remedy for so deep a sore, it behooves Us, Venerable Brethren, to investigate the causes which have engendered it and which foster its growth. . . . We recognize that the remote causes may be reduced to two: curiosity and pride. . . . A lamentable spectacle is that presented by the aberrations of human reason when it yields to the spirit of novelty . . . and when relying too much on itself, it thinks it can find the truth outside the Catholic Church wherein truth is found without the slightest shadow of error [#40].

There are no traditional Masses at Call to Action conventions. However, conference-goers may choose from a galaxy of "prayer experiences"—which are unabashedly "New Age" rituals. The most popular of these, the "Dance of Universal Peace," uses "chant and movement honoring the many spirit-filled traditions of the people of the earth."

At the 1996 CTA convention, people could attend Barbara Papp's "Giving Birth to the Spirit," which "allows the spirit of Jesus to take life within us by focusing on the womanliness of the Mother of Love"; Dorothy Landry's "Earth Ritual: Meditation, Body Prayer, and Sacred Dance," which "centers and grounds the participants in earth, where soul and body are renewed, restored and transformed"; and Julie Howard's "We Are the Circle," in which people "experience the power of the circle through song, movement, shared story and silence." According to Howard, "We are guided to discover God within ourselves, each other, and the circle."

What is the Point of All of This?

Rosemary Radford Ruether reveals the true motivation of many "Catholic" feminists when she described how early feminists hailed the worship of the "Mother Goddess" as part of "the golden age of human society that was overthrown by the regressive influence of patriarchal religion, which displaced an earlier era of women's power." These "spiritual" feminists "sought to revive the ancient matriarchal culture and religion, with its female symbols of the divine, as the more appropriate vehicle for female empowerment."[16]

Feminist dissenting groups often pray to pagan deities. As one of many examples, a favorite chant at Woman-Church "liturgies" is directed towards the Holy Virgin Huntress

Dorothy Landry leads participants at the 1996 Call to Action convention in "Earth Ritual: Meditation, Body Prayer, and Sacred Dance," which "centers and grounds the participants in earth, where soul and body are renewed, restored and transformed."

31

Artemis: "I am good. We are good. I am power. We are power. I am womb-water. We are womb-water."[17]

As comedy writer Dave Barry would say, No, we are *not* making this up.

These feminist groups also jettison the holy saints of the traditional Church calendar and substitute for them pagan and other non-Christian holidays and events such as Kwanzaa, candlemas, eoster (not "easter"), yule, lammas, hallowmas, beltane, solstices, and equinoxes.[18]

A Women's Alliance for Theology, Ethics and Ritual (WATER) manual hints that the members of Woman-Church may someday shed all pretense of having a marginally Christian veneer, and also names as their source of power the pagan "Spirit of Sophia":

> Women-church as an ecumenical experience invites women who have no previous, or at least no recent, affiliation with church to join with other women in search for meaning and value. That is why the influence of so many New Age, Goddess and Native American spiritualities are incorporated with such ease. . . . The worship varies, but sources include Goddess materials, eucharist, chants, songs, poetry, dance and many other creative expressions of women's spirits. . . . It is premature to say whether women-church will remain Christian in focus, but it is important to name its roots as such. . . . As women-church we are well accompanied by one another and by the Spirit of Sophia in our local groups and around the world. This accompaniment is the source of our power. Blessed be.[18]

Sophia (or Wisdom) is probably the most popular feminist/
dissenter substitute for Jesus Christ. A popular card sold at the
1996 CTA convention reads:

> In the beginning was SOPHIA
> Sophia was in God's Presence
> Sophia was GOD
> She was present with God in the beginning
> Through Sophia all things were made
> Apart from Her nothing came to be
> That which came to be in Her was Life
> Sophia became human and lived among us
> And we saw Her Glory
> the Glory that is Hers as God Incarnate
> Full of grace and truth.[19]

Other dissenters and renegade groups state baldly that Christianity—and, indeed, *all* religion—simply has no place in their
lives. The Young Feminist's Network (YFN), organized by the
Women's Ordination Conference, says that "Younger genera-
tions are also more likely than their older counterparts to feel
that it is possible to lead an ethical or moral life without organized religion."[20] "Theologian" Mary Daly goes so far as to rave
that "The myth and symbols of Christianity are *inherently and
essentially* sexist. *Christianity* is idolatry."[21]

Going All the Way

Occasionally, a rock-hard statement of purpose emerges from
the dissenters' reams of warped "femology," psychobabble
and fraudulent history, showing that the authors are deadly
serious about undermining and destroying the One, Holy,
Catholic and Apostolic Church. Ruether's book *Womanguides*
is a perennial favorite of CTAers. The author fumes:

> As women-church we repudiate the idol of patriarchy. . . . Our
> God and Goddess, who is mother and father, friend, lover and
> helper, did not create this idol and is not represented by this
> idol. . . . this idol blasphemes by claiming to speak in the
> name of Jesus and to carry out his redemptive mission, while

crushing and turning to its opposite all that he came to teach. . . . all social reforms superimposed upon our sick civilization can be no more effective than a bandage on a gaping and putrefying wound. Only the complete and total demolition of the social body will cure the fatal sickness. Only the overthrow of the three-thousand-year-old beast of masculist materialism will save the race. . . . No token accommodations will satisfy us. What is required is the *total reconstruction* of God, Christ, human nature, and society. . . . we know we will die unless a WomanChrist pops up (like a rabbit out of a hat) between breasted mountains . . . .

Chillingly, Ruether and other dissenting authors pay homage to Baal, to whom the ancient pagans sacrificed their infant sons and daughters.[22] In *Womanguides*, she gushes, ". . . we see the death of Baal, overwhelmed by the forces of drought and death . . . [the goddess Anath] buries him with rites of mourning. . . . From her sowing of the new wheat in the ground, Baal rises. With a cry of exaltation, we rejoice at the close of the drama: The Lord has arisen, is seated again on the throne. He reigns! Alleluia!"

Ruether's praise of Baal is certainly appropriate in one way: she is stridently pro-abortion.

IV. ASSAULT ON THE "CATHOLIC" CHURCH

"It remains for Us now to say a few words about the Modernist as reformer. From all that has preceded, it is abundantly clear how great and how eager is the passion of such men for innovation. In all Catholicism there is absolutely nothing on which it does not fasten. They wish philosophy to be reformed, especially in the ecclesiastical seminaries. . . . They desire the reform of theology . . . As for history, it must be written and taught only according to their methods and modern principles. . . . a share in ecclesiastical government should therefore be given to the lower ranks of the clergy and even to the laity and authority which is too much concentrated should be decentralized. . . . and there are some who, gladly listening to the teaching of their Protestant masters, would desire the suppression of the celibacy of the clergy. What is there left in the Church which is not to be reformed by them and according to their principles?"

~Pope St. Pius X
Encyclical *Pascendi Dominici Gregis*
("On the Doctrine of the Modernists")
September 8, 1907, #38

What It Means to Be "Universal"

The third of the four marks of the Church is "catholic" (with a small "c"), meaning "universal." The Church is "universal" in the sense that She has Christ present in Her everywhere, with the result that She enjoys "correct and complete confession of faith, full sacramental life, and ordained ministry in apostolic succession" [*Catechism of the Catholic Church*, #830].

Most Catholics are comforted by the fact that, no matter where they travel in the world, the Mass and the Sacraments are always available to them in a recognizable and valid form, and they are able to find priests who are in accord with the Pope and his bishops. This "sameness" throughout the world is a characteristic no other faith has. It is a bulwark and check against fashion and heresy of every stripe.

If professional dissenters manage to enact their proposed "constitutions" and "charters," every parish and every diocese will be unique in its liturgies, practices and beliefs. The catholic (universal) Church will be reduced from uniform belief to a diverse and unruly riot of creeds, thereby fatally injuring its mark of universality.

What It Means to Be "Catholic"

The central meaning of what it means to be authentically "Catholic" is really quite simple to explain. Every true Catholic ardently desires to attain Heaven. We cannot merit Heaven because we are profoundly unworthy of it. We *can* get there, but only through the graces given us as a gift by Our Lord Jesus Christ. The primary channels of His grace to us are the Sacraments. Therefore, every true Catholic cherishes and makes frequent use of the Sacraments.

No Sacraments, no Heaven. What could be simpler?

Dissenters, especially of the feminist variety, do not seem capable of grasping this simple truth because of the pride that blinds them. Not only do they completely reject the Sacraments in their current form, but they have no use whatever for sacramentals such as the Rosary, the Scapular, and holy water, dismissing these as "mere superstition."

In his timeless encyclical *Pascendi Dominici Gregis* ("On the Doctrine of the Modernists"), Pope St. Pius X explained that:

> . . . It is pride which exercises an incomparably greater sway over the soul to blind it and lead it into error, and pride sits in Modernism as in its own house, finding sustenance everywhere in its doctrines and lurking in its every aspect. It is pride which fills Modernists with that self-assurance by which they consider themselves and pose as the rule for all. . . . It is pride which rouses in them the spirit of disobedience and causes them to demand a compromise between authority and

liberty. It is owing to their pride that they seek to be the reformers of others while they forget to reform themselves, and that they are found to be utterly wanting in respect for authority, even for the supreme authority. Truly there is no road which leads so directly and so quickly to Modernism as pride." [#40]

It is this overweening pride that causes dissenters to radically change the source of power and grace in "sacrament" from God to the people. Dianne Neu and Mary Hunt of the Women's Alliance for Theology, Ethics and Ritual (WATER) display this pride when they claim, "From a feminist perspective, a sacrament is an act of lifting to public expression the everyday life of people because such life is holy. Prayer is sustained attention which does not make the divine present, but simply recognizes it as so."[18]

Because dissenters have turned the Sacraments upside down, so that their power flows from people and not from God, there is no need for a priesthood to administer them. And, for them, since priests have become superfluous, there is no need for a hierarchy. Dissenters agitate for a democratic church because, for them, the very meaning of sacramentality is lacking. For instance, CTA speaker Bernard Cooke said: "we still don't know *we are sacrament*. The real presence is ourselves. Bread and wine are only instruments of the eucharist."[23]

What dissenters understand very well is that the structure of the Roman Catholic Church, because it is sacramental, *must* be hierarchical. If it were not, it would degenerate into a riot of competing sects, each with completely different "sacraments." The Church must be hierarchical in order to insure that the Sacraments are administered to as many people as possible in their correct forms.

Dissenters have found that it is extremely difficult to destroy the hierarchy, so they are attacking it indirectly by subverting and diluting the meanings of the Sacraments. They are concentrating their assault on those three Sacraments that have the most immediate impact on those Catholics who still practice their Faith: The Eucharist, the Sacrament of Confession, and the Sacrament of Holy Orders.

37

Reconstructing the Mass

"If they must be Christians, let them at least be Christians with a difference. Substitute for the faith itself some Fashion with a Christian coloring. Work on their horror of the Same Old Thing. The horror of the Same Old Thing is one of the most valuable passions we have produced in the human heart—an endless source of heresies in religion, folly in counsel, infidelity in marriage, and inconstancy in friendship."
~The master demon Screwtape instructing his student demon Wormwood in C.S. Lewis' *The Screwtape Letters: A Devil's Diabolical Advice for the Capturing of the Human Heart*, XXV

Introduction

There are two primary methods by which dissenters hope to remake every parish into a reflection of its members and their attitudes instead of a mirror of the Truth of Christ. These are (1) a complete overhauling of the Sacred Liturgy, as described in this section, and (2) the mandating of "constitutions" down to the parish level, as described in Section II.

The Mass: Center of a True Catholic's Life

The Mass is the focus of an authentic Catholic's spiritual life, and is the most powerful source of Our Lord's sacramental grace. Organized dissenting groups would like to reduce the Mass to a mere collection of "rituals" and "celebrations" centered around various personal and earthly events. For them, the "Eucharist" is not the actual re-enactment of Christ's ultimate sacrifice for us; it is a mere meal, a symbol devoid of sanctifying grace. The Blessed Sacrament is never reserved for adoration at Call to Action conventions, and CTA speakers never mention the "Holy *sacrifice* of the Mass," the "True Presence" or the "Blessed Sacrament." Since the Mass is symbolic to them, dissenters only refer to it as a "liturgy," "celebration" or "eucharist" (with a small "e").

In fact, one feminist nun has gone so far as to state outright that the Mass is not an unbloody re-enactment of the sacrifice of Christ. During her keynote address at the 1997 Catholic Theological Society of America (CTSA) convention, Sister Mary Collins, OSB, (a longtime teacher at the Catholic University of America) said that "a priest-centered theology of the eucharist is defective and inadequate," and that using the word "sacrifice" to describe the Mass means that the actions of the priest are "cultlike."

This outlook inevitably shifts the focus from the limitless power of *God* through His Sacraments to the extremely limited power of *"humankind,"* with all of its imperfections. This would allow the dissenters to easily control the unorganized remains of the Catholic Church. They would also fulfill the prophecy of Romans 1:22-23: "Claiming to be wise, they became fools, and exchanged the glory of the immortal God for images resembling mortal man. . . ."

This Scripture passage, of course, describes Humanism. Pope John Paul II recognized this danger in his Apostolic Exhortation *Familiaris Consortio* [#6]: "History is not simply a fixed progression towards what is better, but rather an event of freedom, and even a struggle between freedoms that are in mutual conflict, a conflict between two loves: The love of God to the point of disregarding self, and the love of self to the point of disregarding God."

The reason given by the dissenters for gutting the Mass is to shift "power" from the hierarchy to the laity. It does not really matter to the dissenters that they will lose the primary source of God's grace, because they truly believe the New Age dogma that "god" is in all of us, and that *we humans* are the source of all holiness.

The Reconstructors

Dianne Neu is one of the foremost "specialists" in reconstructing the Mass.

Immediately after graduating from the Jesuit College of Theology in Berkeley, she founded WATER, the "Women's Alliance for Theology, Ethics and Ritual," a New Age group

Dianne Neu

masquerading as a Catholic theological "think tank." At the 1996 CTA National Convention in Detroit, Neu delivered a talk entitled, "Creating Feminist Liturgies," in which she gave a detailed outline of how she and other revisionists plan to revamp the liturgy.

Neu's reasoning is quite simple. She claims that the current liturgy does not meet the "needs" of the people. Her solution is to institute a system of feminist "liturgies" that will "destroy the patriarchy" by "transferring power from men to women."

"Feminist liturgy brings to public expression the faith life of the community, free from hierarchy, patriarchy, kyriarchy," Neu claims. "It's more than women only, it's supportive men and children who need such liturgies. They're inclusive liturgies, they're feminist liturgies. And I use that word 'feminist' because I think it's important for us to have the edge that we are moving away from the kind of a church that can excommunicate us—that can tell us what we're doing is not 'church.'"

Neu is extremely specific in her plans. She says that New-Age liturgists can use three strategies to "create a feminist liturgy": (1) making a completely inclusive liturgy, (2) reclaiming religious tradition and symbols, and (3) creating new ceremonies.

Many Catholics recognize that these changes are gradually being introduced into their own parishes. Pastors and liturgical directors don't make these aberrations up on their own; they get their ideas, either directly or indirectly, from dissenting groups such as WATER.

Strategy #1: "A *Fully* Inclusive Liturgy"

The purpose of an "inclusive" liturgy is to "empower" all victim groups that believe they have been dominated by or excluded by the Church throughout history. These groups, of course, include women, homosexuals, the "differently abled," and (in practice) anyone who is not a White male.

Neu says that "We speak of 'women first' to signify a power change."

In order to shift power, of course, we must first alter our language. As one example, Neu claims that Haggar was slighted in Scripture merely because she had dark skin. "Darkness gets bad play. There's a power in darkness, there's a womb life in darkness," says Neu. "There's a power in darkness as there is a power in light. We as liturgists need to be careful not to speak of darkness as negative, it's a positive."

Neu has obviously forgotten the chilling words of John's Gospel [3:19-20]: "And this is the judgment, that the light has come into the world, and men loved darkness rather than light, because their deeds were evil. For everyone who does evil hates the light, and does not come to the light, lest his deeds should be exposed." Anyone who embraces darkness, as Neu has, is turning his or her back on Jesus, Who is the "light of the world" [John 8:12].

According to Neu, liturgists should never use words such as "vision" or "hearing" in the Mass because such terms are "ablist," or discriminatory against those who cannot see or hear. She recommends "dreams" as a more inclusive term than "vision." "There's always one more thing to learn in inclusivity," she says. In order to include those of other nationalities, liturgists should use other languages, even if the majority of the people in the congregation don't understand them.

Neu carries "inclusivity" to its logical extreme when she claims that "We all wait for women to have the fullness of our powers used in a recognized [way], in priesthood, I think we need to stretch to a co-papacy, not only a pope that's a woman pope, but we need a decision-making co-papacy involved as well. There's always one more step in inclusivity."

This last sentence warns us that the reformers will never be

41

satisfied until they have completely made God over into man's image, and the Church follows man instead of man following God speaking through His Church. Those misguided Catholics who believe that the feminists will be satisfied with a male/female inclusive lectionary will soon find that their appetite for change is truly insatiable.

Strategy #2: "Reclaiming Religious Tradition and Symbols"

Neu ignores the parameters for the Holy Mass set by Our Lord at the Last Supper, saying that she often uses grape juice instead of wine because she does not want to exclude alcoholics from "eucharist." This single act reduces the Real Presence of Our Lord to a mere symbolic gesture, thereby depriving the Mass of its very sacramentality—and thereby its meaning.

But Neu goes far beyond grape juice, claiming that every group of people should be represented by the form of food and drink used at the "mass." Among her recommendations are harvest bread ("for the harvest season"), cranberry bread, walnut-raisin bread, tortillas ("to celebrate Latin Americans"), nut bread ("for dreamers and prophets"), champagne ("celebrating festivity"), corn bread ("Native Americans and African Americans"), apple juice ("to reclaim women as holy—Eve got a bad rap"), rice cakes (for Asian culture), milk (to celebrate nursing mothers), shortbread (for children), water ("women's lifegiving powers") and saltines (for the "salty elders" among us).

This author, born in Germany, is deeply offended at being excluded by Neu, who did not mention beer and pretzels as "eucharist" in her talk.

Strategy #3: "Create New Ceremonies"

Neu says that liturgists must "[create] new ceremonies that express the spiritual experiences that are absent from the liturgies that you and I know." Under this definition, any significant event in a person's life can be used as an occasion to "celebrate."

Feminist "liturgists" can create "Life Cycle Liturgies," which are rituals for a number of life changes, including menarche (first menstruation), miscarriage or stillbirth, self-insemination or *in-vitro* fertilization (IVF), birth, menopause, and "becoming a crone." According to Neu and her New-Age "crone"-ies, a woman becomes a crone when she is 56 years old, because "the moon of Saturn turns a seventh time."

Liturgists can also replace the Funeral Mass with a death liturgy, because, as Neu alleges, "the Catholic priests don't know what to do with death and dying."

Significantly, feminist "liturgists" can also celebrate abortion if they so desire. Neu emphasizes that "When women make a very difficult choice, the community needs to support that choice. We don't have to make judgment on [whether] the choice is right or wrong, we need to support any one of us who makes the choice for whatever reason."

'Catholics' for a Free Choice (CFFC) is one of the member organizations of the umbrella dissenting group Catholic Organizations for Renewal. Its members often chant, "If men became pregnant, abortion would be a sacrament." Not content with mere chant, CFFC has *already* made abortion into a witchcraft-like "sacrament." A CFFC brochure entitled, "You Are Not Alone" includes two "liturgies" for women who intend to kill their preborn children.[24]

The first "liturgy" is designed to make a woman feel good about the inevitable decision to abort (and there is, of course, *no* question that she *will* abort, none whatsoever). She is to play some soothing background music and "light a candle, absorb its power, and pray." Then she must imagine herself in ten years (a) with a child and (b) without a child. Then she talks about her feelings with an assistant and sings a song entitled "i found god in myself." Finally, she does something "nice for herself" after the "ordeal" of deciding to abort, such as treating herself to an ice cream sundae or a trip to the mall (as many abortion clinics recommend).

Then, of course, there is a "liturgy" for all of those Good Catholic Women who decide that abortion is the Most Moral Thing For Them To Do. The "liturgy" "affirms that a woman has made a good and holy decision [to abort]." Then the "celebrant" and her friends chant the following prayer: "Praised be you, Mother and Father God, that you have given your people the power of choice. We are saddened that the life circumstances of (aborting woman's name) are such that she has had to choose to terminate her pregnancy. We affirm her and support her in her decision." The "celebrants" at the "liturgy" may then express their "sorrow" by "sprinkling flower petals, or sharing dried flowers."[24]

It is significant indeed that CFFC has never developed a "liturgy" for women who decide to keep their babies. This, after all, is the essence of "pro-choice"—there is really only *one* acceptable choice, and that is to abort.

A feminist "liturgist" may also fashion any of a number of "transition liturgies," which mark significant changes in a person's life. These may include rituals that commemorate career changes and moving, loss of friendship, divorce, leave-taking, children leaving home, entering a nursing home, and leaving a religious congregation (a favorite of the members of dissenting organizations).

The third class of ritual is "healing liturgies," which include the marking of the survival of rape, incest, domestic violence, hysterectomies, mastectomies, addictions, HIV, AIDS, and other tribulations.

Finally, the "liturgist" may custom-design a "seasonal liturgy" closely patterned after pagan celebrations, to include ceremonies to honor the harvest, ancestors, or witches. (Neu asks, "Witches really have gotten as bad a press as Eve has. How do we restore witches at Halloween time?")

The primary tools of the above liturgies are centered around circles, fire, candles, water, earth and compost, massage oil, the four cardinal directions, and any other symbol that the "liturgist" sees fit to use.

Significantly, these are primary elements in rituals used by New-Age practitioners and paganists who worship Gaia, the "Earth goddess," and celebrate "her" progression to divinity, a process known as "theagenesis."

Christine Schenk is another of the dissenters who has completely overhauled the meaning of the Eucharistic celebration, changing its source of power from God's grace to [wo]man's feeble attempts at New Age sorcery:

> Eucharist is not really fully eucharist if women are not also able to be included as presiders. . . . we're coming with a different model of eucharist. . . . what we're saying is someone over at St. Elsewhere Parish can say the magic words over the little host and then bring that here to this community where we don't have this holy person who can do the magic, if you will. . . . Another thing that I've heard often from people is that, well, we don't have to worry about who's doing the eucharist, we'll just *have* eucharist. We can do it. We don't need a priest.[25]

Conclusion

Organized dissenters know that they cannot successfully defeat the Church from without, so they burrow away at its structure like termites. As Sister Maureen Fiedler of the Quixote Center says, "Feminists need people with chisels inside, chiseling away at that institution."[26] They know that, in order to destroy the Church, they must attack Her four marks—one, holy, catholic and apostolic.

The most effective and efficient way to attack the universality of the Church is to alter the Mass beyond recognition by destroying its sacramental nature.

Unfortunately, the dissenters have proceeded a long way towards accomplishing this objective in North America and Europe.

Every Catholic who loves Christ and the Mass is duty-bound to oppose this ultimate desecration.

The Sacrament of Confession

"The Church and the sacraments according to the Modernists,
are not to be regarded as having been instituted by Christ Himself.
This is barred by agnosticism, which recognizes in Christ
nothing more than a man whose religious consciousness has been,
like that of all men, formed by degrees. . . . for the Modernists,
sacraments are bare symbols or signs. . . ."
~Pope St. Pius X
Encyclical *Pascendi Dominici Gregis*
("On the Doctrine of the Modernists")
September 8, 1907, #20-21

The Process of Apostasy

Most Catholics who fall away from the True Faith do so gradually. They do not jettison the precepts of the Church all at once; they usually become progressively lazier in one area and rationalize their behavior. Once they adequately justify a particular sin of omission, it is simple for them to excuse others.

This deadly moral lassitude then spreads rapidly until it chokes off any remaining vestiges of fervor. However, they still believe that their "faith" is intact, and many end up in churches that de-emphasize the need for personal salvation and require no personal repentance. Such churches often openly boast that they welcome and accept the person "just as they are." Unfortunately, they go no further; their purpose is to get the *person* to accept themselves "just as they are," and to be "comfortable with their lifestyles."

In almost every case, fallen-away Catholics begin the process of moral disintegration by questioning the need for the Sacrament of Confession.

There is a very logical reason for this, rooted deep in man's fallen nature.

Accepting Sin in Others and in Self

A dissenter's "conscience" is a very flexible entity, similar to incorporeal silly putty, which can easily be twisted into any shape required to cover the sin(s) he happens to be committing at the time. The single most important purpose of this type of "conscience" is to salve the guilt the person is feeling due to his violation(s) of the natural law.

Since the person has accepted these sins in himself, he necessarily becomes "tolerant" of the same sins in others, since to condemn the same sin in others would cause him to be a hypocrite and would make him inconsistent, which is a great sin for liberals.

Therefore, dissenters tend to accept in others whatever sins they practice themselves, even those that are explicitly condemned in Scripture, such as divorce, fornication, adultery and homosexual acts.

The purpose of most dissident groups is to assuage the guilt their members feel by "empowering" them and "affirming" them in whatever sins for which they happen to have a weakness.

The language they use is sympathetic, nonjudgmental, and soothing, and it causes a person to capitulate to weakness and sin instead of fighting it.

Redefining "Sin"

The first step in the process of eliminating the need for personal repentance is to redefine the concept of "sin."

Wisdom 7:17-22 and the *Catechism* [#1849] define sin as "an utterance, a deed, or a desire contrary to the eternal law." Since the eternal law does not change and is universal, the authentic definition of *sin* cannot change and *applies equally to everyone.*

In other words, what is sin for one person is sin for everyone else. We cannot simply decide that our "conscience" standing alone can tell us what is right and wrong. Yet this is precisely what the dissenters attempt to do.

Dignity, an organization of unrepentant Catholic homosexuals, first re-tailors the definition of "sin," then declares that one may disregard Church teaching regarding homosexual activity.

Daniel Helminiak of Dignity claims that, since the person does not *believe* they are sinning, they actually *are not* sinning, and therefore have no need of the Sacrament of Confession:

> As the Catholic Church understands it, wrong and sin are not the same thing. Wrong is harm, disorder, destruction; it is in the objective or external world. . . . Sin is more a general attitude than any particular action. We sin when we deliberately do what we believe is wrong. Then in our hearts we opt for evil. Then we move away from goodness and from God, who is good . . . what you do may really be wrong. But if you don't honestly think so and you do it, well, your heart is not really amiss. . . . Many homosexual people simply cannot believe that gay sex as such is wrong. So they do what for them is "the best they can do," though Church teaching says homogenital relations are wrong. Still, according to the same Church's teaching on conscience, they do not sin in their hearts nor before God. Then they need not confess what is not sin, and they may participate in the Sacraments of the Church.[27]

Similarly, in a brochure entitled "You Are Not Alone," Catholics for a Free Choice (CFFC) claims that "If you carefully examine your conscience and then decide that an abortion is the most moral act you can do at this time, you're not committing a sin. Therefore, you're not excommunicated. Nor need you tell it in confession since, in your case, abortion is not a sin."

This is exactly the kind of thinking that leads to all of the sin in the world today. Under Dignity's or CFFC's way of thinking, a person could easily justify fornication because "I can't control myself"; adultery because "my spouse doesn't understand me"; shoplifting because "they won't miss these little things"; and cheating insurance companies and the Internal Revenue Service because "they can afford it."

Dogmatic Progressives?

The egocentricity of this flexible definition of "sin" may be highlighted by the beliefs and the behavior of the dissenters themselves.

Regardless of what they may say, dissenters are just as

"dogmatic" and "inflexible" as the orthodox Catholics they criticize. They really *do* believe in a form of objective truth, and conscience cannot excuse those who violate their version of "truth."

Take the example of a small child who is raised in a family or community that generally believes that women, minorities, homosexuals and/or Jews are intrinsically inferior and may therefore be exploited. This child grows into an adult who sincerely holds this view and who can easily justify overt discrimination against these groups because his "personal experience" and his "conscience" tells him he may do so.

Would any dissenter allow that this person may freely practice sexism, racism, "homophobia" or anti-Semitism because his conscience tells him he can?

Of course not! According to the "progressive" worldview, the above prejudices are unquestionably sinful, regardless of the sinner's beliefs, background or condition of conscience.

Other "infallible" progressive dogmas include a universal condemnation of both war (even a just war) and environmental irresponsibility.

The Sad Results of No Confession

To eliminate the Sacrament of Confession is to say that we are not accountable to anyone above ourselves, and that we may freely choose whatever course of action feels good or does us good, as long as we can justify it with our "consciences." This is not a truth-based, but a *feeling*-based way of life.

The results of this type of thinking were highlighted at the Call to Action convention and Mother Angelica's Call to Holiness conference in Detroit in November of 1996.

At Call to Holiness, virtually every speaker emphasized the need for personal repentance and conversion. At least two priests were kept busy for hours each day hearing Confessions and giving Catholics advice on how to lead holier lives.

At Call to Action, there was not a single scheduled session of Confession, despite the fact that more than 400 priests attended. Nor was Confession mentioned in any of the nearly 60 talks except in a contemptuous manner. When the author and other orthodox Catholics approached CTA priests and lay members in attempts to discuss the value of Confession, they were frequently met with bemused stares, statements like "You can't be serious!" and lectures on how Confession was part of "The old paradigm" that demanded "submissiveness of some people to others."

Perhaps the dissenters reject Confession because they have to say to a priest, "Bless me, Father, *for I have sinned.*"

Unfortunately, this attitude has infected the American Catholic Church in general, and this is why there is so little Confession and sense of sin today. As Pope Pius XII said, "The sin of the century is the loss of the sense of sin." The agenda of the dissenters has led to this loss.

The Sacrament of Holy Orders

What Do the Dissenters *Really* Want?

N owhere is the Modernist attack on the Sacraments more intense than it is on Holy Orders. For three decades, faithful priests have been under intense pressure to conform to heterodox initiatives, and many weaker priests have systematically self-selected themselves out of the Church.

Orthodox Catholic activists must not for one instant be deluded into believing that the dissenters will be satisfied with married and women priests. Their goals lie far beyond this intermediate step. Their ultimate objective is a complete redefinition of the Mass and of Christ Himself.

The First Step: Married and Women Priests

Dissenters always cloak their language in soothing "cotton candy" vernacular designed to anesthetize the listener and lull him into mental numbness and, therefore, inaction and unawareness. Everything they say sounds so reasonable and seductive— as were Satan's words to Adam and Eve.

Christine Schenk, an agitator for women and married priests, shows that she is a master of soothing language as she pushes her radical agenda: "We believe in a God of abundance, not a

God of scarcity. By confining priesthood to the male celibate variety, we are introducing an artificial scarcity in the Catholic Church. By choosing to do nothing about it, we are saying that the male, celibate priesthood is more important to who we are as Catholics than the Eucharist."[28]

Elizabeth A. Johnson of Parish Renewal Consulting Services (PRCS) goes so far as to say that a male priesthood is not only unscriptural and deadly to the Faith, but can "*unbaptize*" people: ". . . let it be plainly stated that women are icons of Christ, *imago Christi*, in every essential way. . . . To teach otherwise is a pernicious error that vitiates the power of baptism. The native physicalism that reduces resembling Christ to being male is so deviant from Scripture and so theologically distorted as to be dangerous to the faith itself."[29]

Sister Theresa Kane embarrassed Pope John Paul II and all faithful American Roman Catholics during his 1979 visit to the United States when she read a statement demanding the ordination of women priests in his presence. Kane insists that a male priesthood constitutes a form of idolatry:

> We have a responsibility and an obligation to name and proclaim the discrimination that we experience as a form and an expression of idolatry, a modern-day idolatry. . . . In a sense, we have looked upon the male as being the creation of God, and, in a sense, the human representative of God, and what we have truly done is created idolatry, so that at our worship services, when we have services that are predomi- nantly exclusively male, in a sense we're promoting our present-day forms of idolatry. That's truly what we're doing. . . . If only a man can be Pope, if only a man can be a bishop, if only a man can be a priest, that is our present-day idolatry that we're dealing with.[30]

Dissenting groups, including the National Coalition of American Nuns (NCAN) occasionally criticize the nun and priest dolls manufactured by small companies like "Nun-stalgia." At least these dolls reflect a reality, unlike these "woman of cloth" dolls, a popular item at the 1996 Call to Action convention in Detroit.

The Ultimate Objective: Complete Destruction

Modernists claim that they merely want to "rejuvenate," "reform," and "renew" the Church—but their ultimate objective is actually to tear down what they call "the patriarchy," and reconstruct it in their own image, with a pagan goddess at the center. As "theologian" Rosemary Ruether asks: "The Crucified Woman: is she only a victim, or can women bring forth redemption from their sufferings on the cross of patriarchy? . . . no token accommodations will satisfy us. What is required is *total reconstruction* of God, Christ, human nature, and society."[31]

Ruether does not mention what every construction engineer knows: Before you can *reconstruct* something, you must completely *destroy* what stood there before. If the Modernists succeed in this mission, their greatest alleged "oppressor"—the Roman Catholic Church—will not only be defeated; it will simply cease to exist.

Statistical Mendacity

Whenever you hear a liberal quoting numbers in support of his position, you can be certain that he is either ill-informed or lying outright.

Examples of this type of statistical mendacity abound.

Well-known cases include the pro-abortion claim that "5,000 to 10,000 women died of illegal abortions before *Roe v. Wade*"; Dignity's insistence that "ten percent of all people are 'gay'"; and Rosemary Radford Ruether's declaration that "nine million women were burned for witchcraft during the Middle Ages."[32]

Dissenters claim that the priest shortage is caused by mandatory priestly celibacy and the Vatican's failure to ordain women "priests." Then they select large, round numbers at random to buttress their claims, much as pro-abortionists, homosexuals and other anti-lifers have done in the past.

This is a classic example of a liberal strategy that has worked so well many times in the past. Liberals know that they cannot convince the public to accept their programs under normal conditions, so they create a crisis and then ram through their agenda when the public has been frightened and confused enough by their wild claims and bogus statistics.

History gives us many examples of this effective strategy:

● Liberals want free sex and abortion for everyone, including teenagers, but most people don't accept this philosophy. So they publicize a "crisis" in teen pregnancy, give contraceptives to teenagers, and then demand abortion when the teens fornicate more and more and their pregnancy rate skyrockets as a result of the failure of the contraceptives that the liberals gave them in the first place.

● Liberals want homosexuality to enjoy equal moral and legal status with heterosexuality, so they praise and encourage the homosexual lifestyle, condemn any move to control sodomy as "homophobia" and "hate," and then insist on massive government funding and "special rights" laws when AIDS spreads like wildfire.

● Liberals are fearful of the population increase in developing countries, because they believe that a large population means economic power and unwanted competition for the United States, a fear explicitly outlined in National Security Study Memo (NSSM) 200. Therefore, they scare everyone with false statistics about population growth, and demand massive funding for population control programs in developing countries that destroy indigenous cultures and trample human rights on a massive scale, as in Vietnam, India and the People's Republic of China.

Regarding the alleged "priest shortage," dissenters cannot convincingly agitate for acceptance of women "priests" and the discarding of priestly celibacy unless they first convince Catholics that there is a true crisis called the "priest shortage."

While the situation may be serious, it is nowhere near critical enough to even contemplate such measures as the dissenters demand.

As a defender of the true Faith, you should become very familiar with the lies used by dissenters, and you should be able to refute them from memory.

Human Life International's Study on the Alleged "Priest Shortage"

In order to get at the truth regarding this delicate subject, Human Life International researchers compiled more than 40,000 statistics from the 1956 to 1997 issues of *The Official Catholic Directory* and the Vatican's *Statistical Yearbook of the Church* for the purpose of charting historical trends and extrapolating them. These statistics included year-by-year figures for every diocese in the United States, and covered the numbers of diocesan and religious priests, religious sisters, priestly ordinations and numbers of baptized and practicing Catholics.[33]

This section uses the results of this study to examine the main statistical arguments used by dissenting groups, and shows that all of them are completely false.

Therefore, whenever a dissenter uses numbers to substantiate his or her claims regarding women's ordination or priestly celibacy, you should aggressively question his or her statistics.

Without the support of their spurious numbers, the dissenters have no rational support for their positions whatsoever.

Claim #1: "20,000 priests (1 out of every 4) have left the priesthood [in the United States] in the last 25 years, 9 out of 10 to get married."[5,34,35]

Call to Action and other dissenters would like to give the impression that 20,000 men have left the priesthood since Vatican II, most in reaction to the ban on a married priesthood.

The dissenter's statistics are a classic example of "lying by omission."

Vatican statistics show that 22,226 men have left the diocesan priesthood in the United States since 1968; however, *73% of these men left the priesthood because they died.* A total of only 5,950 *living* diocesan priests have defected since 1968 for *all* reasons—an average of about 200 a year—and no numbers are available from any source on the percentage of those who left to get married.[33] In this case, the dissenters are trying to give a false impression here by "padding their numbers" with more than 16,000 deceased priests.

Claim #2: "In another 15 years [2010], there will be only 25,000 [priests]."[36]

As of 1995, there were 48,009 religious and diocesan priests in the United States. In order for this country to lose half its priests by the year 2010, a large asteroid would have to strike the earth.

If trends over the last 20 years continue, there will be about 40,000 religious and diocesan priests in the United States by the year 2010—60% more than claimed by the dissenters.[33]

Claim #3: "By the year 2005 . . . the total number of U.S. Catholics is expected to increase by 65%."[37]

This is the most egregious of the examples of statistical deception used by dissenters, and is completely indefensible.

There were a total of 50.7 million Catholics in the United States in 1986, and there were 56.3 million Catholics in this country in 1996. This represents an average increase of about 1% per year. If this annual growth rate continues, we will have 61.9 million Catholics in the United States by the year 2005—an increase of 10% over the 1996 figure, *not* 65% as the dissenters claim.[33]

In order to fulfill the dissenter's absurd projection that there will be a 65% increase in the number of Catholics by the year 2005, every practicing Catholic family of childbearing age would have to produce 15 children in the next eight years!

Claim #4: "50% of parishes worldwide are currently without resident pastors."[35]

To begin with, the actual number of worldwide parishes without resident pastors is about half of what CORPUS claims, or about 27%. When bandying about this world figure, the dissenters conveniently forget to mention the critical fact that fully two-thirds of the entire world's parishes are located in Europe, where many priests have *always* covered a second small parish with one Sunday Mass that is usually within five miles of their primary residence. If Europe is discounted, only one out of eight—13%—of all parishes in the world have no resident pastor.[33]

The situation in the United States regarding the "priest shortage" is nowhere near as dire as the dissenters say. In this country, there are 18,664 parishes. Of these:

- 87.59% have resident diocesan or religious priests.
- 10.39% are covered by priests from nearby parishes, meaning that a total of 97.98% of all parishes are covered by a resident or non-resident priest.
- Only 1.95% are administered by permanent deacons, men or women religious, lay people, or pastoral teams.
- Exactly 13 parishes in the United States (0.07% of the total) have no priest or administrator whatever, and most of these are in a brief transition period between one pastor and the next.[38]

Claim #5: "Research has shown that at any given time only 50% of priests actually practice celibacy. Three out of every five heterosexual priests in clerical life are in [a] relationship with a woman."[35]

Dissenters can make these claims because they survey *only* men who have already left the priesthood for various reasons, and then falsely assume that the men who remain active in the priesthood have the same sexual habits.

This is as dishonest as finding out that 25% of former convicts have committed armed robbery, and concluding from this that 25% of *all* people have engaged in armed robbery.

In order to demonstrate how absurd the dissenters' claims are, all we have to do is ask ourselves this question: If an active parish priest was the kind of man who would break his vows before God, would he really admit his transgressions to an anonymous person making a telephone survey?

Dissenters make claims that they cannot possibly substantiate, and their footnotes merely refer to other dissenters' writings, never original research. These spurious claims are obviously meant to convince people that even priests who do *not* abandon their vows and leave the Church are living a lie.

The worst aspect of such claims is that they insult and hurt the vast majority of good priests who *do* faithfully keep their vows, and the wide publication of such lies undermines the confidence that the faithful have in Holy Mother Church—and ultimately causes the loss of souls.

Ralph and Linda Pinto of CORPUS downplay the grievous nature of repudiating a vow made before God when they say that "Married priests are not men of broken promises. They are dreamers, they are visionaries, and they are prophets."[8]

Sorry, CORPUS. Any man who makes vows before God and then submits to his own weaknesses and breaks them in order to pursue his own happiness has betrayed the Church, his fellow priests, and those in his flock. Such a man can only be expected to adhere to the watered-down, flexible "vows" concocted by the organization Celibacy Is The Issue (CITI): "I promise obedience (a listening heart), chastity (a loving heart), and poverty (a serving heart). . . ."[39]

The morals of the type of man who abandons his vows, his people and his priesthood (and his attitude towards being a priest) are described in a booklet in which several former priests give reasons for leaving the Church. Former Jesuit Salvatore Giambanco gives this advice: "Date, fool around, have sex, get horny, masturbate, etc. as much as you like once you get out. However, no serious commitments for at least eight months to a year . . . Don't go from one prison to another and then have to go through this whole process all over again."[40]

Judging from an overview of many of the written materials published by the dissenting organizations that oppose the requirement of priestly celibacy, it appears that most men who leave the priesthood do so because they disagree with its stand on sexual morality in areas in which they have weaknesses. Priestly defection due to mandatory celibacy was not a major problem before Vatican II; it only came to the fore when members of the Church (including many priests) began to cater to their own desires instead of submitting to the will of Christ.

Claim #6: "By the year 2005 there will be a 40% decline in priestly vocations [over 1995]."[35]

This is more unsubstantiated propaganda by dissenting groups. The number of diocesan priests ordained in the United States fluctuates widely each year, with 445 ordained in 1986, 635 in 1991, and 420 in 1996. There is a strong current upward trend in diocesan ordinations. If this pattern continues, there will be 624 diocesan priests ordained in 2005—a 50% *increase* over the number of ordinations in 1995, not a 40% *decrease* as CORPUS claims.[33]

Claim #7: "By the year 2000 there will be more married priests in the U.S. than institutionally active priests."[35]

As stated in the rebuttal to Claim #1 above, 5,950 religious and diocesan men have defected from the priesthood since Vatican II, and a total of about 6,800 will have defected by the year 2000. Let us assume for the moment that *all* of these men defected to be married, and that *all* of them are still alive. Given the fact that about 45,000 religious and diocesan priests will be on active duty in the year 2000 in the United States, the number of married priests will be *at most* about 15% of the number of active priests, and probably closer to about 5% to 7%—not *equal* to the number of active priests, as CORPUS claims.[33]

Summary of the Claims

The statistical claims listed above are the primary arguments in a popular CORPUS flyer entitled "ANNOUNCING: Top Ten Reasons Why the Pope Should Allow a Married Priesthood."

Since all of the statistics quoted by CORPUS in the flyer are completely false and misleading, it looks like CORPUS, in the interest of honest "dialogue," had better find a new set of "reasons" for a married priesthood and issue a new flyer.

Whether CORPUS actually does so remains to be seen.

Mathematical and Logical Analysis: Liberalism Causes the "Priest Shortage"

The Analysis

CORPUS, Celibacy Is The Issue (CITI), the Women's Ordination Conference (WOC), and most other dissenting groups either state outright or imply that men are abandoning the priesthood in droves because of the Vatican bans on a married priesthood and women "priests," and an "oppressive, unsympathetic hierarchy" that will not listen to or address their "human needs and wants."

If this allegation were true, we would reasonably expect to see a decline in the numbers of diocesan priests and ordinations of diocesan priests in relatively orthodox dioceses, and an *increase* in priests and ordinations in relatively liberal dioceses. In fact, exactly the opposite is the case.

In the HLI study mentioned above, two clusters of 15 dioceses each were examined over the period 1955 to 1996. One cluster consisted of 15 dioceses that have had a generally orthodox tradition since 1955, and the other cluster consisted of 15 dioceses that have had a generally liberal tradition over the same period.[33]

Figure 1 shows the historical numbers of diocesan priests in these two clusters for the period 1955 to 1996.

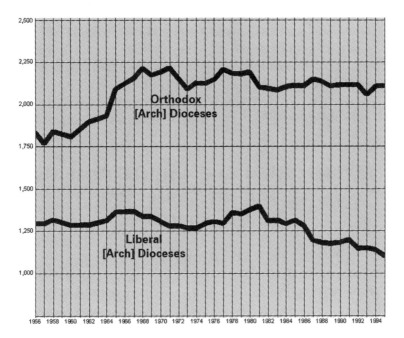

Figure 1. Historical Number of Diocesan Priests Per Million Active Catholics As a Function of [Arch]diocese Orthodoxy or Liberality.

Two patterns immediately become evident upon examining this graph:

(1)   There are currently nearly twice as many diocesan priests per million active Catholics in orthodox dioceses as there are in liberal dioceses (2,057 vs. 1,075); and

(2)   The number of diocesan priests per million active Catholics in orthodox dioceses is remaining steady, while the

number of diocesan priests per million active Catholics in liberal dioceses has been steadily declining for four decades, and probably will continue to do so. In orthodox dioceses, there were 1,830 diocesan priests per million Catholics in 1956, and 12% *more* (2,057) in 1996. In liberal dioceses, there were 1,290 diocesan priests per million practicing Catholics in 1956, and 1,075 in 1996, a 17% decrease.

Figure 2 shows the historical numbers of diocesan priests ordained in these two clusters for the period 1986 to 1996.[33]

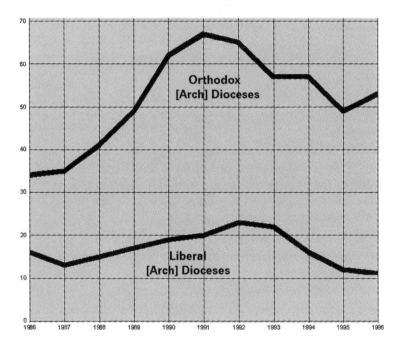

Figure 2. Historical Number of Diocesan Priests Ordained Per Million Active Catholics As a Function of [Arch]diocese Orthodoxy or Liberality.

Two patterns are also immediately evident upon examining Figure 2:

(1)   There are currently nearly *five times as many* ordinations of diocesan priests per million active Catholics in ortho-

dox dioceses as there are in liberal dioceses (53 vs. 11); and

(2)   The number of ordinations of diocesan priests per million active Catholics in orthodox dioceses is experiencing a strong upward trend, while the number of ordinations of diocesan priests per million active Catholics in liberal dioceses was at an anemic level four decades ago and is continuing to decline. In orthodox dioceses, there were 34 ordinations of diocesan priests per million active Catholics in 1986, and 53 in 1996—an increase of more than 50 percent. In liberal dioceses, there were 16 ordinations of diocesan priests per million practicing Catholics in 1986, and only 11 in 1996—a one-third *decrease.*

Logical Analysis

Common sense and a knowledge of basic human nature explains why orthodox dioceses retain their priests and liberal dioceses lose theirs.

After all of the rhetoric on both sides of the conflict, it all boils down to what a priest perceives to be his mission in life.

There is no higher calling for a priest than to work in the vineyard saving souls through administration of the Sacraments and his other skills. A priest who is aware of the true nature of his vocation and the priesthood and sees himself as the bridge between God's grace and his flock does not need to worry about "self-esteem" and "self-fulfillment"; he instinctively knows that he is doing the most important work on earth. He is consecrated. He is unique. He is very special to Our Lady, to the Church, and to the laity who follow him.

A priest who is not aware of or committed to his true role, on the other hand, may possess a conscience numbed by tolerance of many different heresies and sins and will not know where to turn for objective truth. He preaches a watered-down "feel-good" theology designed to avoid offending people. He may have become confused about the differences between the ministerial priesthood and the priesthood of the people, and therefore will think of himself as someone who is not *special*, just somewhat *different* from a lay person. He may accept the dissenters'

62

ultimate goal of transforming the priesthood into a society of "community-ordained facilitators."[4] He may believe the dissenters' propaganda that grace and therefore salvation comes from man, not God, and that people may choose one of many paths to Heaven. Under such a regime of thinking, there is really no difference between a priest and a lay counselor, and the priest himself will fall into sin or heresy, give up the Faith piece by piece, and eventually resolve the conflict between his beliefs and outward appearances by leaving the Church. It is a tragic truth that thousands of priests *have* left the Church, about half to be laicized. Many just walked away, and some did not even leave a forwarding address. Many men who left the priesthood took up a new career of criticizing and attacking the Church, and these populate CTA and similar coventions.

Lesbian agitator Marianne Duddy explains how many priests actually use the *appearance* of priesthood for utilitarian purposes: "It is really important to us [homosexuals] . . . to have friends and co-workers and priests who will go up [to testify]

Marianne Duddy

wearing their clerical collars, even if you never wear it any other time, going to the state house in your clerical collar or your veil if you're a sister—it's *very* powerful stuff. It works, it's a powerful symbol."[41]

In other words, priests and nuns who are ashamed of their ministries, ashamed of their clerical garb, ashamed of *Christ* are hypocritical enough to wear their garb just long enough to gain a political advantage. Such priests and sisters swarm to Call to Action conventions—at the 1996 CTA convention, only a half-dozen of the 1,800 priests and sisters wore their clerical garb or habits, and then only if they were speaking or giving an interview.

Most liberal priests still remain loyal to their vows and their lifelong commitment to the Church. These men remain in the priesthood. However, no such deterrents affect those young men who are considering a vocation. Once again, the difference in rates between ordinations in orthodox and liberal dioceses is stark. Men who are considering the priesthood in an orthodox diocese are impressed with the high calling and sense of mission of the diocesan priests. But those in liberal dioceses have endured years of Catholic schools teaching heresy of every stripe and "feel-good" preaching from liberal priests. Any young man who has the slightest inclination towards orthodoxy will be automatically excluded from the seminary by psychologists and feminist nuns who label him "dogmatic" and "inflexible." Most young men eventually realize that they can find fulfillment in many other lines of work, without the requirement of submitting themselves to vows of chastity and obedience.

This is why the gap in ordination rates between orthodox and liberal dioceses is even greater than the gap in numbers of priests.

Interestingly, the above hypothesis is cross-checked and verified by the fact that liberal churches in the United States have lost an average of 24% of their membership since 1980, while the Roman Catholic Church in the U.S. has *gained* 22% in membership during the same period, primarily because people perceive it as taking strong moral stands on issues that matter to them. Other conservative denominations have gained an average of 30% in membership during the past 17 years.[42]

The Impact of Dissent on Religious Women

Although the situation regarding priests in liberal dioceses is grave, it is nowhere near as serious as the dilemma confronting women's religious orders.

Religious women, of course, were most susceptible to infection by the particularly virulent strain of "Catholic" feminism that appeared in the mid-1960s. After Vatican II, the women's orders began their decline by giving up all the visible trappings of religious life that were labeled "oppressive" or "burdensome" by the liberals, beginning with religious garb, common life and prayer. After abandoning these most distinctive marks of religious life, the sisters found it easy to jettison anything else that did not "empower" them, such as community life and their apostolates, exercised under the authority of the Church. Many women's religious orders, trying to fill the painful spiritual vacuum that resulted, turned to "New Age" philosophies and practices. The moral philosophy of many orders was ruled more by "lived experience" than by the principles of the Church.

Eventually, the women's religious orders simply lost their identities.[43] Young lay women now generally perceive them to be just another group of social service agencies, to be evaluated and then rejected if their benefit packages are less enticing than those of other agencies. And so, fewer and fewer women are interested in replacing elderly and retiring sisters. The total number of religious women in the United States has plunged like a stone: in 1956, there were 180,000 nuns in this country, and now there are only 85,000—a drop of more than 50% in just four decades.

Interestingly, there are still twice as many nuns per million active Catholics in orthodox dioceses as there are in liberal ones (6,659 per million vs. 3,485 per million).[33] Although mother houses have a great degree of control over their sisters, the atmosphere of a local orthodox diocese often moderates their influence.

It is significant that, as soon as documents from Vatican II were approved by the Council, they were distributed to every sister. But other Vatican documents which specifically promulgated orthodox guidelines, such as *Evangelica Testificatio* (1971) and *Essential Elements in the Church's Teaching on Religious Life* (1983) were *not* distributed because, as the liberals said, they were "too divisive" and would have caused splits in the communities.[44] This tactic, of course, is entirely typical of liberals, who in this case preached openness and tolerance while systematically suppressing unfavorable documents for "the good of their orders."

It is obvious that the proportional decline in numbers of sisters far exceeds that of priests. Therefore, one must reflect upon why Call to Action and other dissenting groups place such an extraordinary emphasis on the "priest shortage" while completely ignoring the far more severe "nun shortage." Could it be that the dissenters believe that religious women who remain faithful to their vows are beneath their notice?

Dissenters are not waiting for what they believe is the inevitable; they already own companies that are making priestly vestments for women. Shown is the booth of the company "Companions of Chiara— Vestments for Women" at the 1996 Call to Action Convention.

V. ASSAULT ON THE "APOSTOLIC" CHURCH

"They condemn themselves. We don't have to judge them. They are going to Hell and they are taking others with them. . . . I think one of the problems is that we do not talk about Hell today, and I think that is one of the reasons why so many Catholics are leaving the Church. . . . St. Paul said the dissenters were puffed up with vanity, and spoke only for money, out of their twisted minds. The dissenters have already been condemned."

~Edouard Cardinal Gagnon
President, Pontifical Committee for International Eucharistic Congresses, quoted in *The Wanderer*, September 30, 1993

What It Means to Be "Apostolic"

One Church With One Mission

The Church remains built on the "foundation of the Apostles" and their teachings communicated by Christ, and continues to be guided by them, through their successors in pastoral office (the bishops), until the coming of Christ again. The *Catechism* [#863] says that "The whole Church is apostolic, in that she remains, through the successors of St. Peter and the other apostles, in communion of faith and life with her origin: And in that she is 'sent out' into the whole world. All members of the Church share in this mission, though in various ways."

Every Catholic has been commanded by Christ Himself to "Go therefore and make disciples of all nations . . ." [Matthew 28:19]. We, as members of the Church Militant, do this by confronting and defeating the Culture of Death, not only in front of abortion clinics and porn shops, but within ourselves.

The Role of "Tolerance"

The Culture of Death, through all of the dissenting groups, works perniciously by telling people that they are "just fine the way they are." Dissenters prize nonjudgmentalism and tolerance above all other virtues. Tolerance of diversity can be good, but *only* if the diversity conforms to the will of God. Tolerance of "diversity" in the form of such mortal sins as contraception, abortion and sodomy is a false compassion that can only lead to condemnation, as Proverbs 14:12 tells us: "There is a way which seems right to a man, but its end is the way to death."

The proper course is not to be blindly tolerant of everyone's "lifestyles," but to decide properly what behavior to tolerate and what behavior *not* to tolerate. The members of the Church Militant must learn the difference between virtuous intolerance and non-virtuous tolerance, because the latter is antithetical to the apostolic mission of the Church.

The authentic Catholic must always be intolerant towards sin in himself and in others. It is not enough that we not practice evil ourselves; we have a God-given duty towards others to warn them of their sin. In Ezekiel 3:18-19, God tells us that "If I say to the wicked, 'You shall surely die,' and you give him no warning, nor speak to warn the wicked from his wicked way, in order to save his life, that wicked man shall die in his iniquity; but his blood I will require at your hand. . . . But if you warn the wicked, and he does not turn from his wickedness, or from his wicked way, he shall die in his iniquity; but you will have saved your life."

Needless to say, if Catholics are tolerant of all sin and perverse "lifestyles," the apostolic mission of the Church will be crippled. The Modernist dissenters know this, and have produced two weapons designed to blunt the authentic evangelical message of the Church and replace it with a false compassion: "Dialogue" and small faith communities, as described below.

68

How CTA-Style "Dialogue" Cripples the Church's Apostolic Mission

The Deadliness of Dissenter-Style "Dialogue"

One of the most lethal tactics used by dissenters is the concept of "dialogue." It is so pernicious because it admits of no objective truth, and yields no ground whatsoever on critical issues such as abortion and women's ordination. Its only purposes are to blunt the resolve of activist orthodox Catholics, advance a false ecumenism, and serve as a propaganda tool for the Modernists.

In the Call to Action version of "dialogue," truth is forced to concede that dissent is its equal. In "dialogue," all parties begin with the assumption that nobody is necessarily right or wrong on the issues. Points of disagreement—even those involving fundamental Catholic dogma—are settled by democratic vote.

During these "dialogue" sessions, the parties are not trying to convince anyone of the licitness or truth of their position, but are instead trying to reach an agreement by which all of the parties can co-exist peacefully.

"Dialogue" under such conditions can only lead to agreement on the "lowest common denominator," that position allowing the most personal freedom. For instance, in the "common ground" conferences promoted by pro-abortionists and some pro-life activists, the fundamental issues—the humanity of the preborn child, its soul, the issue of killing—are off-limits, so the "woman's right to choose" wins by default.

Eternal and Neverending Debate

Since CTA-style "dialogue" admits to no objective truth and limits the scope of the debate, it leads to eternal wrangling over such tangential issues as the role of conscience. And so, central issues such as women's ordination and priestly celibacy are left unaddressed and unresolved, which gives the dissenters the "wiggle room" they need to continue their agitation. "Dialogue" also gives them the additional benefit of being able to give the impression that even the orthodox Catholics who are talking to them believe that there is room for systematic dissent in the Church.

And so, no authentic progress is ever made because the central issues are never resolved. The issues that were being addressed by "dialogue" back in 1976 are exactly the same issues that are being discussed today. In this manner, "dialogue" with dissenters is actually *counterproductive* because it insists upon debating questions that have already been decisively settled and is therefore a waste of time for everyone involved. This is why "dialogue" with hardened dissenters is antithetical to the Church's apostolic mission. Joseph Cardinal Ratzinger highlighted this critical shortcoming when he explained that "The notion of dialogue . . . becomes both the quintessence of the relativist creed and the antithesis of conversion and the mission. . . . Only if I suppose in principle that the other can be as right, or more right than I, can an authentic dialogue take place."[45]

As far as the dissenters are concerned, as long as there is not *unanimous consent* on an issue, it can never be resolved. Sister Fran Ferder said that the issue of priestly celibacy "is still open . . . Based on what Cardinal Martini of Milan said in his interview last year, the question is still open."[46] And Edwina Gately asked at the 1996 CTA convention in Lincoln, Nebraska, "How can anything be final, be finished, be definitive, when scientists tell us that 90% of the cosmos is a mystery?"

This is an illogical and inconsistent position. Ferder, of course, would not agree that the question of racial equality is "still open," despite the fact that a few racists believe that anyone who does not possess blue eyes and light skin is inferior.

So why do the dissenters continue to push "dialogue" if they know that the fundamental issues will never be resolved?

Call to Action-style "dialogue" is, quite simply, a subterfuge. Instead of promoting unity, it continually brings up settled questions and will *continue* to bring them up until they are finally settled to the *dissenters'* satisfaction. At that point, of course, the concept of "dialogue" will be discarded because it will have served its purpose. Many orthodox Catholics know from bitter experience that the most uncommunicative and authoritarian people of all are dissenters who have power— particularly in chancery offices all over the country.

Is Authentic Dialogue With Dissenters Even *Possible?*

Just because dissenters abuse and exploit a method of communication doesn't mean it should be discarded out of hand. Authentic dialogue between parties with different beliefs is possible if it is understood that the purpose of the exercise is to seek truth, not accommodation, and progress, not compromise. All of those involved in dialogue must acknowledge that there are basic truths that are beyond debate and must be accepted by all parties. As Bernard Cardinal Law has said, "The Church already has 'common ground.' It is found in Sacred Scripture and Tradition, and it is mediated to us through the authoritative and binding teaching of the Magisterium."[47]

It must also be understood that the objective of authentic dialogue is to make the Word of God and His truth more widely known. True dialogue cannot be based upon one's personal opinions or experiences, or it degenerates into a contest of anecdotes and therefore produces nothing.

The Role of Small Faith Communities

"This people honors me with their lips, but their heart is far from me; in vain do they worship me, teaching as doctrines the precepts of men."
~Jesus Christ, quoting the prophet Isaiah
Gospel of Matthew 15:8-9

Why SFCs?

While they "dialogue" with activist Catholics, dissenters do not neglect marginal Catholics who do not know their Faith. They have invented the ideal mechanism for "weaning" these Catholics away from the "hierarchical" Church: "Small faith communities" (SFCs) or, as they are

71

sometimes called, "house churches."

Father Art Baranowski explains the purpose of SFCs: "We must begin again as church, reinvent the church, re-found the church—with a different structure and leadership. Small faith communities are no longer an option but a necessity. . . . The refounded parish will be formed of clusters of communities relating regularly with the home church under the direction of parishioner leaders. . . . This new model of church is happening all over the world."[48]

The SFC Process

Another dissenting priest, Father Ron Purenowski, believes that radical Catholics must begin by restructuring parishes into communities or "house churches" of 8 to 12 people each. These parishioners initially sign up for meetings to hear a particular speaker, and after several meetings, they begin to relate more strongly to each other. During this period of time, an experienced dissenter has been watching the group and has identified those Catholics who are most likely to be anti-authoritarian and revolutionary in their thinking.[49]

He or she presents these selected people with the prospect of organizing a "house church." They continue the process of "weaning" away from the parish by evolving into a permanent group, and elect leaders that connect them to the parish in a superficial manner. Gradually they weaken their tenuous bond with the home parish and the Church, develop their own unique variety of prayer life, rituals, and even beliefs, and complete the process by developing into a small alternative "house church" whose purpose is not to worship and glorify God, but to give a supportive environment to each of its members.[49]

It is entirely possible that such a "house church" could be comprised solely of hard-core pro-abortionists who act as clinic escorts for a local abortuary, or promiscuous homosexuals who hold their meetings in a "gay" bar. The people participating in such a groups could adopt any morality or beliefs they liked, since they acknowledge no higher authority.

Activist dissenters see small faith communities as fertile ground for experimentation, where they may try any liturgical or dogmatic "innovation" without having to fear the prying eyes of the "hierarchy." According to CTAer Virginia Hoffman, SFCs are "not authoritarian . . . [they are] completely participatory." She says that "We're all a priestly people called upon to continue his ministry in the world, which is not primarily offering sacrifice in the Temple, but a change in the perception. . . . acting out a different vision of church is how the revolution happens, and house-church is one of the places that does it." Dissenting priest Father Bill Callahan revealed that the SFCs will be used as an agent of change in the Church, and that dissenters will then attempt to inject these changes back into the Church: "It is important for these communities to move forward with married priests, with women priests."[36]

These "small faith communities" or "house churches" are ultimately meant to be a replacement for the Church, and may partially explain church closures in some liberal dioceses.

SFCs are a refinement of the "small faith sharing groups" envisioned in the RENEW Program, which itself was developed by Archbishop Peter Gerety, an organizer of the original 1976 Call to Action convention in Detroit.

It is obvious that CTA-style small faith communities are antithetical to the apostolic mission of the Roman Catholic Church because they cause people to turn in towards themselves instead of directing their energies outwards towards evangelizing the world. Every dissenting SFC will be as unique as the beliefs of its members, and in no case will these beliefs reflect those of the One True Faith or further the cause of evangelization of the world.

There Are Many Causes for Hope

To be a dissenter from the One True Faith is to live in a world that is unrelievedly depressing. Modernists create discouraging statistics on the "priest shortage" out of thin air, and talk endlessly about oppression, patriarchy, and the empowerment they so desperately crave.

But this is the distinctly limited *human* way of looking at things, not the Godly way. We cannot measure the health of the Catholic Church purely with graphs and numbers and statistical trends (although, as Section IV shows, these are encouraging). The work of the Holy Spirit does not conform itself to human standards.

So, in the midst of widespread dissension, we have a flourishing diocese in the middle of the plains of Nebraska; while liberal seminaries stand virtually empty, the Legionaries of Christ have a huge number of qualified applicants; while many Catholic children are traumatized and scandalized by explicit sex education programs, hundreds of thousands of Catholic homeschooled children are receiving instruction in the True Faith from their parents; and Catholic families are working together and flocking to flourishing communities like Steubenville, Ohio, and Front Royal, Virginia, to defend the Faith.

There are many signs of the apostolic zeal and unquenchable energy of the emerging Roman Catholic Church in America sprouting up everywhere.

Conclusion

As those who travel it well know, the road to Heaven is not an easy one. It is often steep and winding, and frequently littered with obstacles to the Faith. Because of these difficulties, the Church has erected guardrails in order to keep the faithful on the road to Paradise. Beyond the guardrails lie many dangers—the high cliffs of apostasy, the impenetrable thicket of moral relativism, and the deep, swift rivers of Modernism.

Since they cannot distinguish between licit and illicit freedoms, dissenters see the guardrails not as a safety measure, but as a barrier. They not only want to pass beyond the guardrails, they want to tear them down so that other souls will more easily stray from the path.

Our job as evangelizers for the Culture of Life is to warn people of the dangers that lie beyond the guardrails.

VI. TACTICS OF THE DISSENTERS AND HOW TO DEFEAT THEM

"Further, none is more skillful, none more astute than they, in the employment of a thousand noxious devices; for they play the double part of rationalist and Catholic, and this so craftily that they easily lead the unwary into error; and as audacity is their chief characteristic, there is no conclusion of any kind from which they shrink or which they do not thrust forward with pertinacity and assurance. . . . The Modernist sustains and includes within himself a manifold personality; he is a philosopher, a believer, a theologian, an historian, a critic, an apologist, a reformer."
~**Pope St. Pius X**
Encyclical *Pascendi Dominici Gregis*
("On the Doctrine of the Modernists")
September 8, 1907, #3, 5

Introduction

Dissenting organizations and individuals employ tactics that have been proven to work in chanceries and parishes all over the United States and all over the world. These time-tested methods are extremely effective when used against ill-informed and unorganized lay people and priests.

A Catholic who is serious about being a member of the Church Militant has a high duty to defend Her from those who would destroy Her. As soldiers of Christ and protectors of the True Faith, you must become very familiar with all of these tactics. You should be able to quickly identify the methods of the dissenters when you see them, and then take quick action to expose them and stop them in their tracks.

This section describes the most common tactics used by dissenters and the most effective ways of defeating them.

Tactic #1:   The Appeal for Tolerance

The most common tactic used by dissenters is an appeal for tolerance and nonjudgmentalism. Many dissenters know only one Scripture passage: "Judge not lest ye be judged."

The reason dissenters love tolerance so much is that they have become accustomed to their own sins and the sins of others. This is why they emphasize the perfect mercy and kindness of Jesus Christ while forgetting His perfect judgment; why they tend not to believe in Satan and Hell, except as earthly metaphors; and why they have completely lost any sense of sin.

Our Lord has instructed us to hate sin and love the sinner. St. Paul admonished Titus to "Rebuke them sharply that they may be sound in Faith" [Titus 1:13]. Orthodox Catholics do not judge dissenters as individuals, because only God knows the state of a person's soul. We must steadfastly judge *sins* and *heresies* in general, and exhort those guilty of them to repent. Our job is to "Go therefore and make disciples of all nations ... " [Matthew 28:19], and this may very well include helping back into the Church those disciples who have lost their way.

In order to rescue the dissenters, we must boldly and clearly proclaim apostasy, heresy, abortion, sterilization, homosexual relations, contraception, divorce and other evils to be gravely sinful. Scripture tells us that we must reach out to those in sin or *we ourselves will be judged guilty because they are lost.*

As previously described, God tells us in Ezekiel 3:18-19 that we have a *duty* to warn the wicked, and, if we do not do so, their condemnation will be on our heads.

Dissenters also frequently speak of "love." What is true love: To allow others to travel unhindered down their wide and smooth road to Hell and eternal damnation, or to try to turn them from their path? Would we rather be their friends on *their* terms and see them condemned, or would we rather be their friends on *God's* terms and spend eternity with them in Heaven? We should remember, when fighting dissent, that it is not "us versus them"; it is instead *"all* of us against the Devil."

To *tolerate* sin is to *accept* sin and surrender to our fallen natures. We must cast out the Devil and his works wherever we find them, whether they be in ourselves or in others. To do otherwise is to turn our backs on our roles as Christ's disciples— and means abandoning and betraying those who need us the most: the dissenters.

Tactic #2: Mixing Lies with the Truth

Local dissenters will frequently organize parish or diocesan events which mix orthodox Catholic speakers with those holding heretical views. They do this in order to confuse the faithful and give themselves a veneer of legitimacy.

When challenged, they will often claim that they are trying to be "inclusive of a variety of viewpoints."

This is a hypocritical and inconsistent assertion, since Call to Action would *never* allow Mother Angelica or any other ortho- dox Catholic to speak at *its* events. This duplicity is typical of dissenters. At CTA's founding convention in Detroit in 1976, it ruthlessly shut out and ridiculed orthodox speakers even while extolling the virtues of "inclusivity," and this tradition of *exclu- sivity* has continued to the present day.

A barrel of high-quality grain with a little poison in it is still poisonous. Dissenters work just like the Father of Lies, the Devil: They proclaim truth laced with heresy and lies. Pope St. Pius X said of them, "Although they express their astonishment that We should number them amongst the enemies of the Church . . . they proceed to diffuse poison through the whole tree, so that there is no part of Catholic truth which they leave untouched, none that they do not strive to corrupt" [*Pascendi Dominici Gregis*, #3].

Catholics have been confused by this tactic for many years, and it is time for us to stand up and say "ENOUGH!" Anyone who suspects that dissenters are coming to speak to their parish or diocese should contact a Catholic organization dedicated to defending the Faith in order to find out the speaker's viewpoints.

These organizations are listed in Section VII.

If an outside speaker is a known dissenter, orthodox Catholics should document this fact as completely and as early as possible and present the evidence to the pastor, bishop or event coordinator, demanding that the dissenter's invitation be revoked. Make sure that the person making this decision knows that he or she has a clear choice between authentic Catholic doctrine and heresy, and make certain that the decision-maker knows that his or her decision will be carefully observed and widely publicized. If the person delays giving his or her answer for a long period of time (a common tactic), or refuses to disinvite the dissenter, local orthodox Catholics can take many courses of action. These include contacting the local secular press, picketing and leafletting the event, videotaping the dissenter's talks, carrying protest signs into the event, and asking the dissenter difficult questions. If enough controversy arises from the event, the diocese or parish will think twice before inviting another dissenter to speak.

The bottom line is this: Orthodox Catholics must no longer tolerate dissent in their parishes and dioceses, and must send a very clear message that the dissenters will encounter organized and effective resistance wherever they go. Do not apologize for being "exclusive"; *truth by its very nature is exclusive*, because it must be intolerant of lies.

Tactic #3:   Labeling and Stereotyping

The vast majority of dissenters have a double standard: They demand tolerance while offering none. They declare that they are inclusive, yet systematically exclude viewpoints other than their own, and they claim that they are "nonjudgmental," even as they harshly judge and ridicule orthodox Catholics.

In order to confuse lay people and boost their own morale, dissenters frequently stereotype and ridicule orthodox priests and activist lay people, including the Holy Father, whom they label "timid," "fearful," "out of touch," "harshly legalistic," and "arch-reactionary." Their publications are saturated with disrespectful stereotyping of those people who do not agree with them.

It is useful for orthodox Catholics to know how the dissenters see themselves and those who adhere to the authentic Catholic Faith. In her talk at the 1996 CTA National Convention, dissenter Nancy Westmeyer said that:

> [Words that describe patriarchy] include control, lone ranger, controlled, "right-way" answers, dictator, unequal, fear, pushed, dominated, suspicion, limitations, closed, selfish, dead-end, loneliness, monologue, frustration, lack of respect for persons, deficiency, divisive, angry, aggressive, defensive . . . they reflect our experience of patriarchy . . . the partnership ones are consensus, togetherness, listening, willingness, recognition of gifts, affection, process, assertive, energizing, wisdom, feminine, understanding, trust, relational, peace, justice, spirit, humor, discernment, support, humility, mutuality, mutual respect, collaborative, honesty, communication, openness, acceptance, freedom, equal, respect, caring, vulnerability, creativity, shared power, we, communion, affirmation, participation in decision-making and accountability.[50]

One of the most powerful weapons used by dissenters is the showcasing of active priests and lay people who have fallen into sin and are therefore acting inconsistently with Church teachings. Orthodox Catholics can use this tactic as well, by showing that dissenters do not practice what they preach when they speak of "tolerance," "nonjudgmentalism" and "inclusivity."

Tactic #4: The Plea for Dialogue

As described in Section V, dialogue with dissenters is completely useless because they believe in no objective truth. Any time a faithful Catholic sits down and "dialogues" with dissenters, he is wasting his valuable time. Dissenters see "dialogue" as a tool to extract concessions from orthodox Catholics that will cripple their ability to fight heresy, and to distract attention from critical issues. Any orthodox Catholic who "dialogues" with apostates and does not concede important points to them should expect to see himself and his organization ridiculed and labeled "rigid" and "obstructionist" in the apostate's next newsletter.

Tactic #5: Ignore Church Law and Customs

Every liberal social movement has broken the law on a wide scale in order to project an image of principle and courage. If the authorities crack down on the liberals, they immediately assume the victim cloak and proclaim their fellows to be martyrs; if the authorities do nothing, the liberals claim that the law is useless and the behavior in question should be legalized because it is "happening anyway."

Whenever true Catholics take action against dissenters, the resulting crescendo of sniveling and vituperation can be almost deafening. After a half-dozen orthodox Virginia Catholics were dragged out of their *own church* by police for protesting a Call to Action function there, the dissenters whined that "It is outrageous that mainstream Catholics are being treated as pariahs by a group of radical, right-wing idealogues who resemble nothing so much as the Brown Shirts of Nazi Germany."[51]

Dissenters have taken a page from the abortionist's playbook and are flouting Church law and tradition on a wide scale. Father Bill Callahan is explicit as he explains this tactic: "The [Church] system is showing such strains and contradictions that it is ready to crumble. Systems crumble much more readily if there are people marching around the walls, everyone with a little rock pick, working on their part of the wall! You can't repel them all."[36]

Louise Haggett, founder of Celibacy Is The Issue (CITI), describes the process that the dissenters are encouraging: "In the Catholic Church, practice becomes custom, and custom becomes law. If you look at the recent history of altar girls, the Vatican had initially said no, but people ignored that and had them anyway and eventually that changed the law. That's what I think will happen with married priests."[52]

Whenever the dissenters want to make "progress," they simply ignore everything but their own desires, particularly in the area of the liturgy. In a manual published by the Women's Alliance for Theology, Ethics and Ritual (WATER), Dianne Neu and Mary Hunt say that "Women are co-celebrants in some services whether they are ordained or not. In some Catholic churches, the congregants, especially women, are saying the

Eucharistic prayer with the priest whether they are invited to or not."[18]

The only possible response that orthodox Catholics can take to this kind of agitation is to stand firm in the tradition of St. Augustine and not give an inch. The dissenters may ridicule us and call us names like "Nazis," and liberal pastors may even have us arrested and dragged away, but thousands of Saints have suffered far more in defense of the Faith, and we should model ourselves after them.

Tactic #6: Exclusion of Diverse Viewpoints

Dissenters say that they operate with love and tolerance for everyone, but this is simple propaganda they use to cover a systematic policy of exclusion.

Throughout all history, dissenters and apostates have ruthlessly excluded all orthodox voices when they attain control in a certain area. Call to Action and its "sister" dissenting groups are no exception. At the original 1976 Call to Action convention in Detroit, the dissenters tried their best to prohibit orthodox Catholics from speaking. When they could not accomplish a complete ban, they ridiculed, mocked and booed the traditional Catholics when they spoke.

This policy of systematic exclusion continues. For example, the "Women-Church Convergence" is dedicated to "celebrating the diversity of Catholic women." At its April 1997 "Weavers of Change" conference in Albuquerque, WCC boasted that "The meeting will offer more than 30 varieties of Sunday worship— including Goddess worship, an Indian pipe ceremony, Sufi dancing, a Holocaust remembrance, a Quaker meeting and a feminist eucharist." When someone proposed to include a normal Mass with a male priest to make traditional Catholic women feel included, the person was booed and her plea was rejected.[53]

VII. WHAT CAN *I* DO?
HOW TO GET RID OF DISSENTERS IN YOUR PARISH AND DIOCESE

"Therefore, having this ministry by the mercy of God, we do not lose heart. We have renounced disgraceful, underhanded ways; we refuse to practice cunning or to tamper with God's word, but by the open statement of the truth we would commend ourselves to every man's conscience in the sight of God. And even if our gospel is veiled, it is veiled only to those who are perishing. In their case the god of this world has blinded the minds of the unbelievers, to keep them from seeing the light of the gospel of the glory of Christ, who is the likeness of God. . . . We are afflicted in every way, but not crushed; perplexed, but not driven to despair; persecuted, but not forsaken; struck down, but not destroyed; always carrying in the body the death of Jesus, so that the life of Jesus may also be manifested in our bodies.
~2 Corinthians 4:1-4,8-10

Getting Started

Every faithful Catholic is deeply concerned about what is happening in the Church today, not only in Canada and the United States, but all over the world. The Catholic Church is actually under siege by those who would undermine or even destroy Her most basic dogma and teachings.

Unfortunately, concern alone will not safeguard the Faith. Decisive *action* by a large number of priests and lay people is also required if the Church is to persevere. Father John Hardon, S.J., said at the 1996 Call to Holiness conference that "The Church cannot be destroyed, but let's be clear: the Church in any particular country *can* be wiped out. We have some 1,900 extinct dioceses in the world today. Barring a miracle of grace, one diocese after another in the United States will disappear."

There are many things a single Catholic can do to defend the One True Faith, and these actions fall into two general categories. You can either confront the dissenters directly, or, if for some reason you cannot do this, you can support those who are battling on the front lines.

This section includes a number of suggestions for fulfilling your role as a member of the Church Militant. These proposals are only a starting point; anything you can do to get rid of the baleful influence of the Modernist dissenters is precious in the eyes of God and Holy Mother Church.

If you feel called to fight dissent in your diocese or parish, you must first prepare yourself, because you will be stepping onto the most difficult battlefield of them all. You must develop a vigorous prayer life if you do not already have one. You must organize, and then you must learn how to defend the Faith steadfastly. Finally, as a soldier of Christ, you must learn the dissenters' tactics and how to stop them cold.

Only *then* will you be ready to step onto the battlefield.

Pray!

First of all, every true Catholic must *pray for Holy Mother Church* and her faithful priests and religious. The battle between the Culture of Life and the Culture of Death is like an iceberg; the visible part of the struggle is only a small portion of the conflict. The vast majority takes place in the invisible supernatural sphere. Prayer for the general intentions of the Church and the Holy Father is essential to the success of our temporal efforts, and prayer for specific intentions regarding the defense of the Faith is also most efficacious.

In particular, we should remember that the most powerful enemy of Satan and his minions is the Mother of God, Mary Most Holy. Our prayers to Mary, particularly on behalf of Pope John Paul II, who has such devotion to her, cannot go unanswered.

Keep in mind that the Holy Sacrifice of the Mass is the most powerful prayer of all. If you can, try to attend at least one weekday Mass a week, and offer intentions for the conversion of specific dissenters.

Organize!

Seasoned campaigner Edmund Burke once said that "When bad men combine, the good must associate [with each other]; else they will fall one by one, an unpitied sacrifice in a contemptible struggle."[54]

Never has this been so true as in the struggle for the heart of the Roman Catholic Church in America. A single person who raises his or her voice in opposition to heresy, schism and apostasy will quickly be crushed under a tidal wave of ridicule, condemnation and vituperation; but a *dozen* well-organized true Catholics or, better yet, a *hundred* with truth on their side will be an obstacle that even a liberal diocesan hierarchy will be unable to ignore or overcome.

You can either organize your own parish or diocesan group, or you can affiliate yourself with one of the national Catholic organizations that are fighting dissent and other attacks on the Church. These organizations are listed below.

Adoremus Society for the Renewal of the Sacred Liturgy
Post Office Box 5858, Arlington, Virginia 22205
Telephone: (703) 241-5858, FAX: (703) 241-0068
Newsletter: *Adoremus Bulletin*

Catholics United for the Faith (CUF)
827 North Fourth Street, Steubenville, Ohio 43952
Telephone: (614) 283-2484 or (800) 693-2484

Human Life International (HLI)
4 Family Life, Front Royal, Virginia 22630
Telephone: (540) 635-7884, FAX: (540) 636-7363
Web site: http://www/hli.org
Newsletters: *HLI Reports* and *HLI Special Reports*

Keep the Faith
810 Belmont Avenue, Post Office Box 8261, North Haledon, New Jersey 07508
Telephone: (201) 423-5395

Roman Catholic Faithful, Inc. (RCF)
Post Office Box 109, Petersburg, Illinois 62675
Telephone: (217) 632-5920, FAX: (217) 632-7054
Web site: http://www.rcf.org

St. Joseph Foundation
11107 Wurzbach, No. 601B, San Antonio, Texas 78230-2570
Telephone: (210) 697-0717
Newsletter: *Christifidelis*
Provides assistance to orthodox Catholics whose rights have
been violated by dissenting groups or their pastors or bishops.

Please keep these organizations in your prayers, because they
are on the front lines of defending the Faith.

Whatever course of action you take, it is essential to have an
experienced dissent-buster speak to your group in order to train
it in strategy and tactics. If you do not have outside expertise,
you are much more likely to fail in your mission, because the
struggle between truth and dissent at the diocesan or parish level
is fraught with pitfalls and concealed obstacles. You may even
be able to bring in several speakers and hold a mini-conference
open to the public, which would be a great recruiting tool. After
the conference, you could have the speakers instruct the leaders
of your group during a confidential session in the art of thwart-
ing dissent.

It is also absolutely necessary that you have an orthodox
priest as your spiritual advisor. When you finish your preparation phase and step out to fight the dissenters, you will encounter
spiritual obstacles you never dreamed existed. A good priest can
help you get through these difficult times and can help you
prepare yourself for the abuse and ridicule you are likely to
suffer. He can help you avoid the bitter and complaining nature
that some orthodox Catholics fall prey to, and can instead help
you become an optimistic and effective fighter for the Faith.
Additionally, the priest can give you insight as to diocesan and
parish politics when you need such information.

Really Learn Your Faith!

Do you know how to confidently and accurately answer a dissenter who claims, "We can use birth control now, because the Vatican said that we can use our consciences in the *Declaration on Religious Freedom*?" Can you clearly explain the Church's "double effect" principle as it applies to abortion for the mother's life and to sterilization? Can you convincingly demonstrate *why* the Church cannot ordain women to the ministerial priesthood?

If you can do all three of these, congratulations—you are among the select group of only about *one percent* of Catholic laymen who can do so.

These are the issues you *will* encounter when you fight dissent on any level. You will not just hear them from professional dissenters and agitators; you will also hear them from friends, family members, fellow parishioners, and even uninformed priests.

In Hosea 4:6, God laments that "My people are destroyed for lack of knowledge."

Learning how to defend the Faith is a difficult process, but is mandatory if you are to be effective. The best way to do this is to study the *Catechism of the Catholic Church* in detail, with the same level of attention as you would give a college course. It is best to study by yourself and then meet on a weekly basis for a couple of hours with the other members of your dissent-busting group to strategize and discuss difficult concepts and how to explain them clearly.

This process may take a year or more, but it will transform you into a much more effective soldier for Christ.

Learn the Battlefield!

You cannot be an effective soldier for Christ unless you know the topography of the battlefield. Educate yourself about the Church's situation. You can do this by reading good books on dissent, learning about its origins, history and current forms. Then you can become familiar with the current situation in the Church by subscribing to one or more of the journals which are dedicated to fighting dissent and promoting the truth. The idea behind all this reading is to familiarize yourself with both the theory behind dissent and current news and trends in the Church.

There are literally hundreds of magazines and journals devoted to fighting abortion, euthanasia, the homosexual rights movement, pornography, population control and other evils. When fighting dissent, you should instead subscribe to orthodox journals and magazines that specialize in this area or at least address it on a regular basis. These include:

The Catholic Answer
Our Sunday Visitor, Inc., 200 Noll Plaza, Huntington, Indiana 46750; Telephone: (210) 356-8400
Issued bimonthly; $18 annually.

Catholic World Report
Post Office Box 591300, San Francisco, California 94159-1300
Telephone: (800) 651-1531
11 issues per year; $39.95 annually.
In-depth reporting on specific attacks on the Faith around the world.

Crisis
Post Office Box 10559, Riverton, New Jersey 08076-0559
Telephone: (800) 852-9962, e-mail: crisis@catholic.net
11 issues per year; $29.95 annually.
A mixture of short articles and current news and trends in the Church.

Envoy
Subscription Department, New Hope, Kentucky 40052-9989
Telephone: (800) 553-6869
Web site: http://www.envoymagazine.com
11 issues per year; $28.99 annually.

Fellowship of Catholic Scholars Quarterly
Box 495, Notre Dame, Indiana 46556

First Things: A Monthly Journal of Religion and Public Life
Post Office Box 3000, Department FT, Denville, New Jersey
07834; Telephone: (800) 783-4903
10 issues per year; $29 annually.
Several long articles and book reviews in each issue, along with
Father Neuhaus' observations on religion and public life.
Past issues are available on *First Things'* Web site at
http://www.firstthings.com.

HLI Reports and *HLI Special Reports*
Human Life International, 4 Family Life, Front Royal, Virginia
22630; Telephone: (540) 635-7884, FAX: (540) 636-7363
Web site: http://www.hli.org/
Issued monthly; $30 annually for each.

Homiletic and Pastoral Review
Ignatius Press, 2515 McAllister Street, San Francisco, California
94118; Telephone: (800) 651-1531
11 issues per year; $24 annually.

Human Life Review
Editorial Office, 215 Lexington Avenue, 4th Floor, New York
City, New York 10016
Issued quarterly; $20 annually.
A fine scholarly journal, with several long articles each issue by
leading orthodox Catholic scholars.

Inside the Vatican
St. Martin de Porres Lay Dominican Community, New Hope,
Kentucky 40052-9989
Telephone: (800) 789-9494, FAX: (502) 325-3091
Issued monthly; $49.95 annually.

National Catholic Register
Post Office Box 5158, Hamden, Connecticut 06518-5158
Telephone: (800) 421-3230, FAX: (203) 288-5157
e-mail: cmedia@pipeline.com
Issued weekly; $49.95 annually.
Not to be confused with the ultra-liberal *National Catholic Reporter*, this newspaper keeps up on current trends in the Church and often features articles on dissent and dissenters.

New Oxford Review
1069 Kains Avenue, Berkeley, California 94706
Telephone: (510) 526-5374, FAX (510) 526-3492
Issued 10 times per year; $19 annually.

Sursum Corda!
Foundation for Catholic Reform
Subscription Department, 1331 Red Cedar Circle, Fort Collins, Colorado 80524; Telephone: (970) 483-8781
Issued quarterly; $26.95 annually.
Family-oriented magazine with short articles and current news in the Church.

This Rock
Post Office Box 17490, San Diego, California 92177
Telephone: (888) 291-8000, FAX (619) 541-1154
Web site: http://catholic.com/rock/thisrock.htm
Issued monthly; $29.95 annually

Voices, Voices, Voices
Women for Faith and Family, Post Office Box 8326, St. Louis, Missouri 63132
Telephone: (314) 863-8385, FAX: (314) 863-5858
e-mail: 72223.3601@compuserve.com

The Wanderer
201 Ohio Street, St. Paul, Minnesota 55107
Telephone: (612) 224-5733.
Weekly; $40.00 annually.
This weekly newspaper is the best available source for specific

and very timely information on dissent in the American Catholic Church. *The Wanderer* is not afraid to name names!

Orthodox books that examine the subject of dissent in detail include the following. You may be able to find these in your local public or diocesan libraries, but don't count on it. Your dissent-busting organization may wish to purchase these books and pass them around among your members. In order to keep up with the latest offerings, make sure that you subscribe to catalogs from orthodox book publishing companies such as:

- **Christendom Press**, 134 Christendom Drive, Front Royal, Virginia 22630, telephone: (800) 877-5456.
- **Ignatius Press**, Post Office Box 1339, Fort Collins, Colorado 80522, telephone: (800) 651-1531.
- **Keep the Faith**, 810 Belmont Avenue, Post Office Box 8261, North Haledon, New Jersey 07508 telephone: (201) 423-5395.
- **Neumann Press**, Route 2, Box 30, Long Prairie, Minnesota 56347, telephone: (320) 732-6358.
- **Our Blessed Lady of Victory Mission**, Rural Route 2, Box 25, Brookings, South Dakota 57006-9307, telephone: (605) 693-3983.
- **Our Lady's Book Service**, Servants of Jesus and Mary, Post Office Box 93, Constable, New York 12926, telephone: (800) 263-8160.
- **Roman Catholic Books**, Post Office Box 2286, Fort Collins, Colorado 80522-2286.
- **Sophia Institute Press**, Box 5284, Manchester, New Hampshire 03108, telephone: (800) 888-9344.
- **Tan Books and Publishers**, Post Office Box 424, Rockford, Illinois 61105, telephone: (800) 437-5876.

Some of the most detailed books written by orthodox authors on the dissent movement include:

- Monsignor George A. Kelly. *Keeping the Church Catholic with John Paul II.* Order from Ignatius Press. Interesting background and history of the Church mechanism for decision-making, and detailed information on dissent and the battle for the soul of the Church, particularly with regards to contraception and obedience to the Pope.

- Father Vincent P. Miceli. *Women Priests and Other Fantasies.* Order from Keep the Faith, address given above. The author examines the pandemonium that results in the Christian Church (particularly the Catholic Church) when the senses of the sacred and supernatural are lost. The instant that Holy Scripture is judged by secular standards, the message of Christianity is hopelessly compromised and lost.

- Father William Oddie. *What Will Happen to God? Feminism and the Reconstruction of Christian Belief.* Order from Ignatius Press. The Neofeminists are striving to eliminate from all church documents and prayers what they consider to be "sexist" language. Father Oddie exposes the fallacies of this goal, and shows what will happen if we allow radical feminism to continue to dictate to the Church. The elimination of so-called "sexist" language is only the beginning!

- Donna Steichen. *Ungodly Rage: The Hidden Face of Catholic Feminism.* Order from Ignatius Press. A very detailed and absorbing account of how the Roman Catholic Church in the United States has been infiltrated and subverted by Neoliberals and Neofeminists for the express purpose of blunting its effectiveness in its reaction to evils such as divorce, abortion, and euthanasia. Much detailed information on many dissenters and dissenting organizations, with an emphasis on feminist and "New-Age" groups.

- Hans Urs von Balthasar, Joseph Cardinal Ratzinger, Walter Kasper, *et.al. The Church and Women: A Compendium.* Order from Ignatius Press. A collection of articles by leading Church scholars on the role of women in the Catholic Church today and contemporary issues regarding feminism, including the ordination of women and the role and importance of the family. The role of women is developed in a context faithful to Scripture, tradition, and the Magisterium of the Church.

- Dietrich von Hildebrand. *The Devastated Vineyard.* Order from Sophia Press. The author describes in harrowing detail the destruction of the Roman Catholic Church in America and in Europe, and the methods of infiltration and subversion now being used to confuse and paralyze all conservative Christian churches in our country today.

Use the Web

The amount of information on the World Wide Web (WWW) is equivalent to the information in all of the libraries in the United States today. You can find virtually any piece of information in any field, and you do not even have to leave the comfort of your home or office if you are connected to the Internet.

You can visit the Web sites of more than one hundred orthodox Catholic organizations for information and encouragement. Those sites that specifically deal with dissent and other attacks on the Catholic Church as primary or secondary topics include:

Catholic Answers: http://www.catholic.com
Catholic Civil Rights League: http://www.catholicleague.org
Envoy Magazine: http://www.envoymagazine.com
Eternal Word Television Network (EWTN): http://ewtn.com
First Things Magazine: http://www.firstthings.com
Human Life International (HLI): http://www.hli.org
Roman Catholic Faithful (RCF): http://www.rcf.org
This Rock: http://www.catholic.com/rock/thisrock.htm
The Vatican: http://www.vatican.va/

You may also visit the dissenters' Web sites to gather information and intelligence. Many times, they will publicize information on events that will happen in your area months before your diocese or parish advertises them. If you are looking for information on a particular dissenter or group, you can also use the Yahoo! search facility at http://www.yahoo.com/ to search for them.

Association for the Rights of Catholics in the Church
    (ARCC): http://www.astro.temple.edu/~arcc/
Call to Action (CTA): http://call-to-action.org/
National Catholic Reporter: http://www.natcath.com/search/
Pax Christi: http://www.nonviolence.org/pcusa
We Are Church Coalition (WACC):
    http://www.listserv.american.edu/catholic/referendum/

Know the Dissenters' Tactics

Become intimately familiar with the dissenters' tactics, because every diocese and almost all parishes have experienced them. As an orthodox Catholic activist, you can derail the dissenters' plans with a surprisingly small amount of organization and effort—but *only* if you can anticipate them.

Subscribe to their newsletters. Visit their Web sites. Become familiar with their language and theories. Make sure that you know how to refute their propaganda and their slogans, such as their inevitable charges that orthodox Catholics are "divisive."

Finally, learn their primary tactics, which are described in Section VI.

Since dissenters work by stealth, your job is to raise their profiles, turn a spotlight on their activities, and then defeat their attempts to infiltrate your diocese or parish.

Support Faithful Men and Women Religious

If you, as a lay person, often feel lonely and isolated in your beliefs, imagine how much worse it must be for priests or sisters who are isolated and shunned by their own close-knit communities because of their orthodox beliefs.

Many faithful priests feel isolated and alone in their own dioceses because they are attacked by "progressive" laity and sometimes even by their own bishops whenever they preach or teach the truth regarding such "hot-button" topics such as abortion, divorce, homosexuality and pornography. Frequently they are even ridiculed or silenced for defending the basic tenets of the Faith, such as the True Presence, and sometimes they are even forced into early retirement. Orthodox religious sisters can often feel even more isolated as their orders and mother houses speed unhindered down the feminist road to extinction.

These men and women need to know that they have the support of the laity who still believe. They need to see with their own eyes that there is a strong and growing movement towards the restoration of the True Faith, for this will reinforce their hopes.

You can invite faithful priests, sisters, brothers and deacons to your home for dinner and a few hours of relaxation. You can commend them and their work in letters to the diocesan newspaper, to your bishop, and, most importantly, face-to-face. If you share a common interest with a religious person, you can take him or her along the next time you go hiking, bicycling, picnicking or camping.

Maintain the Right Attitude

As a dissent-buster, there are several things you must be. **You must be immune to discouragement.** The dissenters exist because they cause concern among Catholics by constantly exaggerating the problems in the Church. Remember that their motives are the deconstruction/

destruction of the Church, and that things are nowhere near as bad as they say. Also keep in mind that there is an ongoing revival in the Catholic Church today, and *you* can be a vital part of it. Above all, remember 1 Corinthians 15:58: "Therefore, my beloved brethren, be steadfast, immovable, always abounding in the work of the Lord, knowing that in the Lord your labor is not in vain."

You must be eternally watchful. Examine the catechetics and sex education programs in your Catholic schools, keeping in mind that any program, no matter how orthodox, can be changed on the spot by Modernist teachers with an agenda. The only way to ensure that your children are raised chaste and faithful is to be certain that the school they attend is completely orthodox, or to teach them yourself at home—something that half a million families are doing in the United States today.

Don't be lulled into complacency by the fact that two-thirds of all Call to Action members are over 50 years of age, and that CTA is obviously not doing a good job of recruiting from the young. Keep in mind that these are the people who are still infected with the iconoclastic mood of the 1960s and therefore continue in their activism. Modernism and indifferentism are not high ideals that young people want to fight for, and so they are not replenishing the ranks of CTA and other dissenting groups. Instead many youth simply live lazy, spiritless lives, which is just as dangerous to their Faith as outright dissent.

You should also keep an eye on the literature rack in your church. Dissenting groups often manage to establish a "beach-head" there, because the pastor doesn't have time to read everything that goes in the rack. Read the literature yourself, and if it contains dissent, or if it is produced by any of the groups listed in Appendix B, show your pastor the problems in doctrine or dogma and ask him to remove the material. If he refuses, ask him in the name of "diversity" to include authentic Catholic literature. If he denies *this* request, you will know that you have a typical close-minded liberal for a pastor, and you may have to take measures such as leafletting the church.

Finally, **you must be prepared to go for the long haul.** Many chanceries are infested with dissenters who have held their positions for many years and may seem to be almost unassailable because of their many connections and because their bishop may be afraid to take them on. You should accumulate information on these people and let them know that you are carefully watching them. This alone will usually make them less brazen in their dissent. Above all, remember that if you watch enough, document enough, agitate enough and pray enough, the toughest and most entrenched dissenter will eventually go down.

If you have a particular complaint that receives a negative response or no response from your pastor or bishop, you may want to take the matter up with higher authority. There is a specific procedure you must follow if you want to be certain that your protest will be properly attended to at higher levels. You can get this procedure, entitled "Effective Lay Witness Protocol," from Catholics United for the Faith, 827 North Fourth Street, Steubenville, Ohio 43952, telephone: (614) 283-2484 or (800) 693-2484.

Think Papally, Act Locally

A soldier would never be sent into an armed conflict without intense and appropriate training. You, whose work is infinitely more important, will be ready to step onto the battlefield only after you have established a firm foundation of prayer, organized with other orthodox Catholics, and learned your Faith and the tactics of the dissenters. It may take you a year or more of preparation before you are ready to act; but do not become discouraged. The better prepared you are, the more effective you will be as a soldier in the eternal struggle between the Culture of Life and the Culture of Death. Your spiritual advisor and seasoned dissent-busters will be able to help you determine when you are ready to engage in battle against the Modernists.

A Final Note: The Impact of Dissent on the Pro-Life and Pro-Family Movements

What's the Connection?

Some Catholic pro-life and pro-family activists don't really understand why they should be involved in fighting dissent in their dioceses and parishes, since this activity seems to be unrelated to the critical work they are doing. Similarly, those who fight dissent often believe that anti-abortion activism, while important, is not relevant to what they are doing.

Even though pro-lifers and dissent busters must naturally focus on their own areas of activism, they must understand that the attacks on the family and on the Church are intimately connected.

The Indirect Connection

The Roman Catholic Church is almost alone in its opposition to the vast litany of sins that are sweeping across the globe today, killing tens of millions of people and capturing tens of millions of souls. Pope John Paul II and a handful of cardinals and bishops from various countries are virtually the only leaders speaking out against the evils of abortion, contraception, population control, divorce, sodomy and pornography.

If the dissenters succeed in their mission to blunt or muffle the prophetic voice of the Church, there will be virtually no resistance to their agenda. *All* pro-lifers—not just Catholics—will find themselves far more isolated than they are now, and their fight against abortion will be made far more difficult. For this reason, pro-lifers of all faiths should support *all* of those denominations speaking out against the many evils of our age.

The Direct Connection

Father John Hardon, S.J., has called this century the "Age of Martyrs," since more Catholics have been murdered for their beliefs over the last hundred years than in any previous century.

There have also been more *unborn* Catholics slaughtered by abortion across the world in the last 30 years than the number of martyrs in all previous centuries *combined.*

Since 1966, there have been 37.9 million legal *surgical* abortions in the United States.[55] Catholics for a Free Choice and other pro-abortion groups say that Catholic women abort their children at the same rate that other women do. Sadly, this claim is true.

This means that 8.6 million Catholic babies have been aborted since 1966. Among these babies would have been 1 cardinal, 57 archbishops and bishops, 6,760 priests, 12,320 sisters, 1,660 permanent deacons, and 850 religious brothers.[55] Every week, 15 to 20 future priests, sisters and brothers are thrown into dumpsters behind abortuaries around the nation. Meanwhile, Call to Action and its fellow dissenting organizations approve of this slaughter under the pretense of "freedom of choice."

The persecutors Darius and Diocletian could never have imagined such an effective attack upon the hierarchy and the people of the Church.

If such a slaughter of religious men and women and lay Catholics had taken place in the open, there would have been a worldwide cry of protest. However, since every murder by abortion takes place behind clinic doors and is committed by men and women who never have to raise their voices, nobody notices. And, since this slaughter is all carried out in the name of the god "choice," few dare interfere.

It is revealing to see how directly abortion impacts the Catholic Church. Fourteen states legalized abortion in this country before *Roe v. Wade.* An examination of the number of baptisms in these states shows that baptisms were rising steadily in each state until just before surgical abortion was legalized. On the average, baptisms in these states dropped an average of 28% after abortion was legalized—a percentage that is almost

Conclusions

identical to the ratio of Catholic women obtaining abortions.[33,56] In a very real manner, those who defend the Faith are fighting abortion, because they are speaking out against the root causes of abortion and all other evils: modernism and indifference to the message of Christianity. And those who fight abortion are effectively defending the Faith, since they are saving the lives of many future Catholics, including those of men and women religious not yet born.

Both groups of activists should work more closely together, since such cooperation renders both movements more effective. Their missions are not mutually exclusive; they are complementary.

VIII. SUMMARY AND CONCLUSIONS

*"Now the works of the flesh are plain: Fornication, impurity,
licentiousness, idolatry, sorcery, enmity, strife, jealousy, anger,
selfishness, dissension, party spirit, envy, drunkenness, carousing,
and the like. I warn you, as I warned you before, that those who do
such things shall not inherit the kingdom of God.
But the fruit of the Spirit is love, joy, peace, patience, kindness,
goodness, faithfulness, gentleness, self-control;
against such there is no law."*
~Galatians 5:19-23

The Marks of the Church

The Roman Catholic Church is "one" in Faith and "one" in sacrifice, has one sacramental system, and has one divine head (Christ) and one earthly head (the Pope).

The Church is "holy" in Her Founder, Jesus Christ, in Her teachings, in Her means of providing grace (the Sacraments), and in the many members who follow Her teachings and use the means of grace She provides.

The Church is "catholic" or universal in that She is the church of all nations and races.

The Church is "apostolic" in that She can trace Her origin in an unbroken line back to the Apostles on whom Christ founded the Church.

No other church possesses all four of these marks.

And, if the dissenters have their way, *no* church will possess all four of these marks.

The dissenters seek to subvert the "oneness" of the Church by enacting "constitutions" and "charters" at all levels that will splinter the Church into a hundred thousand separate and distinct sects. They admit that they are not leaving the Church because they hope to tailor Her teachings to accommodate their own sins and shortfalls.

They wish to ruin the "holiness" of the Church by enacting a universal shift in emphasis from personal to corporate sin, thereby eliminating the need for personal repentance in favor of making people feel accepted "just as they are."

They are attempting to destroy the "catholicity" of the Church by attacking the very fountain of grace that flows to us through the Sacraments. To dissenters, the source of "grace" is not God, but man, and so they are focusing their attacks primarily on the Sacraments that faithful Catholics have recourse to most frequently—the Eucharist, Confession, and Holy Orders.

Finally, they want to completely blunt the "apostolic mission" of the Church by absorbing the evangelical zeal of Catholics in fruitless "dialogue" and by setting up tens of thousands of "small faith communities," each with its own unique beliefs and customs.

The Attributes of the Church

The chief attributes, or qualities of the Church, are Her authority, infallibility, and indefectibility.[57] If the dissenters succeed in enacting even a relatively small portion of their agenda, these qualities will be completely obliterated.

The authority of the Church means that the Pope and the bishops, as the lawful successors of the Apostles, have the power from Christ Himself to teach, to sanctify and to govern the faithful in spiritual matters. It is quite obvious that the dissenters refuse to accept any authority above their own personal experience. As Sister Miriam Therese Winter asserted during the 1996 national CTA convention, "The primary source of God's word is not the Bible, but life. We have to liberate God's word from the bondage of the book, from the linear and the cognitive . . . *Whatever experience you feel, that is God.* We are ordained to a ministry of justice and peace, we have to reimagine and reinvent everything."

The infallibility of the Church means that She, by the special assistance of the Holy Spirit, cannot err when She teaches a doctrine of faith and morals. However, the dissenters claim that there is no objective and unchanging truth, and that all things must be interpreted in light of present needs and wants. Therefore, there is no such thing as an "infallible" truth.

The indefectibility of the Church means that She will continue to exist as Christ founded Her until the end of time. The dissenters are fond of quoting John Stuart Mill, who said "My love for an institution is in direct proportion to my desire to reform it." Therefore, by the dissenters' strange logic, anything you truly "love" can never be left alone; it must constantly be changed. Not even the Sacraments are safe from their tampering.

By Their [Rotten] Fruits
You Shall Know Them . . .

Whenever an orthodox Catholic bishop, priest or lay person fails to be absolutely perfect in some way, or appears to be inconsistent in any manner, dissenters invariably sneer "by their fruits you shall know them."

The most wonderful gifts we can receive are the fruits of the Holy Spirit. Dissenters have rejected these fruits and have instead greedily clutched the decaying and corrupting "fruits" of Satan. Even the most cursory examination of their speeches and writings show that they have displaced love with selfishness; joy with dejection and anger; peace with endless, aimless agitation; patience with an unquenchable desire for immediate gratification; kindness with intolerance and judgmentalism; goodness with corruption; faithfulness with fickleness; gentleness with harshness; and self-control with self-indulgence.

The ultimate objective of the organized dissenters is not to *give*, but to *take away*. They want to take away the Rock of Peter and smash it into dust. They want to take away the Sacraments and force every Catholic to depend upon his or her own minuscule powers. And they want the Church to stop preaching and teaching the truth so that they will feel accepted in our world.

As bad as things appear at times, we should remember the eternal words of Cicero in *Familiares*: *Alios ego vidi ventos; alias prospexi animo procellas* ("I have already seen other winds; I have already beheld other storms"). The Church has always fought Her enemies and has always triumphed and endured, because the Holy Spirit guides Her, even when Her people go astray.

And She will continue to endure until the end of time. Christ Himself has made this promise to us.

There are signs of promise all over the country and all over the world. It can only be thus when the dissenters exterminate their own children while orthodox Catholics nurture large families. Things are getting darker no more—the light is getting brighter, and so the contrast is sharper.

More and more Catholics are asking themselves the question: "Do I want to be an American Catholic or do I want to be a Roman Catholic American?"—and taking the latter course.

But this latter course requires action. James 4:17 tells us that "Faith without works is as dead as a body without breath."

Which course will *you* take?

L'OSSERVATOIR SAN FRANCISCO

January 22, 2019 **Feast of St. Margaret Sanger**

Pope Joan II Wraps Up Busy Week; "Looks Forward to Time with My Lover"

Following a whirlwind fundraising tour for the International Planned Parenthood Federation, Pope Joan II returned to San Francisco yesterday and delivered a homily on her new encyclical *Insensate Verbum Errorum*, which resolved many of the theological and dogmatic questions that have been plaguing the World catholic Church for decades. This landmark document rejects the idea that "god" is a male, and it teaches that "Jesus Christ" was only a gifted human prophet of his time, many of whose teachings are not really relevant to our modern age. It also jettisons the absurd idea that he was born of a virgin, a concept that Pope Joan acknowledges "flies in the face of all modern medical knowledge and human experience."

In other action, Pope Joan delivered excommunication orders against 152 dissenting Catholic groups, ranging from the Apostolate for Family Consecration to the Zanesville, Ohio, Catholics United for the Faith chapter. The Holy Crone said that "I strongly dislike using a punishment that was abused by the patriarchal hierarchical church, but I really had no choice. This action will send a strong message to these divisive dissident groups that we will no longer tolerate their obstructionism. These people must learn that Jesus Christ was a prophet of tolerance and compassion, not of judgmentalism." The 152 named organizations had loudly and sometimes obnoxiously opposed many of the initiatives of the World catholic Church, despite the fact that their complaints had already been rejected unanimously by the Supreme Council of the Church.

A recent public opinion poll by Catholics for a Free Choice shows that 97% of American catholics agreed with the Pope's assertion that "These issues have been settled for two decades now. The Church has pronounced on them many times, and it is absolutely ridiculous that these dissenters continue to insist that the deposed former Pope, John Paul III (aka Francis Arinze), not the church matriarchy, has the answers."

In other activities, Her Holiness canonized 12 new saints, bringing the total to 2,251 during her six-year co-papacy. These included St. Pamela Maraldo, St. William Brennan, St. Theodore Kennedy, St. Charles Curran, St. Matthew Fox and St. Frances Kissling. This action was accomplished after she ordained 51 new priests who had completed the rigorous three-week training program administered by the Women's Alliance for Theology, Ethics and Ritual (WATER) Ovulary in Washington, D.C. This program emphasizes feminist theology and herstory, how to create meaningful eucharistic and other rituals, and how to be inclusive and tolerant, all necessary for a clergyperson. "This is one of the best classes we've had in years," enthused Pope Joan. "They exactly reflect the minority makeup we want in our practitioners, with proportional numbers of gays, women, and those of other faith traditions, such as Buddhists, Taoists, Moslems and Hindus." Pope Joan said that the ongoing policy of declining to ordain men will continue for at least another three years, until the World catholic Church attains a proper balance between the six genders in the priesthood at large.

In other news, the American catholic Church matriarchy pledged to double the budget for its longstanding program of subsidizing voluntary pregnancy interruptions, sterilization, family planning and sex reassignment surgery for minority women and men, and the World Council of Catholic Bishops (WCCB) announced plans to mandate its new sex education program which teaches, among other things, that "the only sexual perversion is virginity."

106

The WCCB also allocated 31 million New World Dollars to the continuing task of converting the former Vatican City into a monument intended to commemorate the longstanding oppression of millions of women and gays throughout the world. "I know this seems like a lot of money," said Pope Joan, "but it's essential that the people remember what can happen when you concentrate too much power in too few hands without sharing it. This is why I am having talented women and gay artists chisel the words "NEVER AGAIN" one million times into the stone of St. Peter's Basilica and into the flagstones of St. Peter's Square."

After her busy week, the Holy Crone said that "I look forward to spending some quality time with my lover. These six-hour work days are just killing me. She's looking forward to it as well. While I am gone, the co-Pope, Joan Chittister, will take over. We've already discussed some exciting new initiatives that we'll announce next week that will further bring the Church into the 21st Century. . . . "

The above fictional news article from the equally imaginary *L'Osservatoir San Francisco* is a preview of one possible future for Holy Mother Church if the "Constitution" and "Charter" of the Association for the Rights of Catholics in the Church (ARCC) are enacted and enforced by Vatican III. The article may at first seem disorienting or perhaps even completely improbable.

But don't be fooled. All of the events described in the above "news article" are either stated or implied objectives of ARCC and other dissenting groups and would be entirely possible under their reign. Highly educated liberals are debating some of the other items, such as whether there are six or seven genders.

If you would like to see the Roman Catholic Church transformed in this way, then you need do nothing at all, and it *will* happen. A prophetic saying attributed to Edmund Burke holds that "All that is required for evil to triumph is for good men to do nothing."

If this article disturbs you, it is your *duty* to oppose the agenda of the dissenters. See Section VII for suggestions on what *you* can do to stop these events from happening.

APPENDIX B
PARTIAL LIST OF DISSENTING ORGANIZATIONS

"Your organization is intrinsically incoherent and fundamentally divisive. It is inimical to the Catholic faith, subversive of Church order, destructive of Catholic Church discipline, contradictory to the teaching of the Second Vatican Council, and an impediment to evangelization. Of course, your slogan, which you claim to have from the mouth of Pope John XXIII, is not relevant to the issues at hand, since neither you nor your group possess the competence, ability or authority to determine authentically what is essential or nonessential in Catholic doctrine, Catholic moral teaching, or Catholic Church law."
**~March 18, 1996 Letter of Fabian Bruskewitz,
Bishop of Lincoln, Nebraska, to Lori Darby and
John Krejci, co-chairmen of Call to Action Nebraska**

Fifty years ago, when you heard that an outside speaker was coming to your diocese or parish, you could be certain that your bishop or pastor had taken the time to insure that the person was orthodox in his or her views. And you could take it on faith that the literature in the back of your church would uphold Catholic doctrine.

Sadly, this is not the case today.

Dissenters work primarily by stealth. They attempt to infiltrate heretical speakers into conferences. They also place their poisonous tracts into church literature racks without the pastor's permission or thorough review. When they are exposed, they say that they "didn't know" and invariably appeal to the pastor's or bishop's sense of "tolerance" and "diversity."

The first step in fighting dissent is to *find* it. This can be difficult, because professional dissenters are expert at the art of camouflaging their viewpoints, and mixing their noxious brew of 90% truth and 10% lies.

The most efficient way to battle dissent is to simply shut it down without discussion. You can do this by refusing to allow *any* speaker from a dissenting group to air his or her views in your diocese, and by rejecting *all* books and literature authored by dissenters.

This Appendix consists of a list of about 200 dissenting groups whose speakers and publications should be rejected out of hand.

Keep in mind that this is by no means a complete list; there are new dissenting groups and "small faith communities" (SFCs) popping up almost weekly. The only way to be certain that a speaker is orthodox is by checking on his or her background; the only way to be certain that a piece of literature authored by an unfamiliar person or group is orthodox is by reading it carefully.

Since dissenters commonly work by infiltration and stealth, their groups often possess obscure names which give no indication as to their functions or degrees of heterodoxy, e.g. the "James Markunas Society," the "Sea of Faith Network," "WIT" or "Keryx."

National headquarter cities are noted below for some organizations in order to aid in identification, since sometimes the names of several groups are nearly identical. See page 116 for a description of the codes that appear at the end of each entry.

Adrian Dominican Sisters, Adrian, MI [C]
American Catholic Church [F]
American Catholic Lay Network (ACLN) [M]
Aquinas Institute of Theology, St. Louis, MO [C]
Association for the Rights of Catholics in the Church (ARCC) [A,C,F,I,J,K,N]
Association of Pittsburgh Priests, Pittsburgh, PA [F]
Bear & Company [M]
Bear Tribe [M]
Benedictine Sisters of Erie, Erie, PA [C]
Black Sister's Conference (BSC) [M]
Bread for the World, Detroit, MI [C]
Bread Rising, Minneapolis, MN [F]
Brothers and Sisters in Christ (BASIC), Blackrock, Ireland [F]
Brothers for Christian Community, Warren, MI [B,F]
BVM Network for Women's Issues [E,M]
Cabrini Mission Corps, Radnor, PA [F]
Call for Dialogue on the Future of Priestly Ministry [C]

Call to Action (CTA) [A,B,F,I,J,K,M,N]
Canadian Network for Women's Equality (Canada)
Canon Law Society of America (CLSA) [M]
Carmelites of Indianapolis, Indianapolis, IN [C]
Catholic Advocates for Equality (CAE) [M]
Catholic Coalition for Gay Civil Rights [M]
Catholic Common Ground Center, Long Beach, CA [B,F]
Catholic Gay and Lesbian Family Ministry [H]
Catholic Organizations for Renewal (COR) [F]
Catholic Parent's Network (CPN), Baltimore, MD [F,H]
Catholic Reform, Albert Lea, MN [F]
Catholic Theological Society of America (CTSA) [L,M]
Catholic Women for Reproductive Rights (CWRR) [M]
Catholic Women's Network, Sunnyvale, CA [D,F]
Catholics Act for ERA [M]
Catholics Against Capital Punishment, Arlington, VA [F]
Catholics for a Changing Church (CCC), Great Britain [F]
Catholics for a Free Choice (CFFC) [A,C,E,F,G,I,J,M]
Catholics for Renewal, Saverton, MO [F]
Catholics for the Common Good [M]
Catholics for the Spirit of Vatican II [F,I]
Catholics of Vision (COV) (Canada)
Catholics Speak Out (CSO), Hyattsville, MD [A,F,I,J,K,M]
Celibacy Is The Issue (CITI) [A,F,I,J,N]
Center for Action and Contemplation, Albuquerque, NM [C,F,H]
Center for Arts & Spirituality, Hudson, NH [F]
Center for Education and Enlightenment (CEE), Lexington, KY [D]
Center of Concern (COC), Washington, DC [F,M]
Central American Religious Study Group [M]
Central American Telephone Tree (CATT) [M]
Chicago Catholic Women (CCW) [E,G,M]
Chloe's People, Hayward, CA [F]
Christenrechte in der Kirche (Germany) [N]
Christian Faith Committee, Washington, DC [D]
Christic Institute [M]
Church of Reconciliation [F]
Church on the Move (Europe)
Church Women United (CWU) [M]
Clare's Well [M]
Coalition of Concerned Canadian Catholics (CCCC) [A,B,F,I,J,N]
Coalition of Concerned Catholics (CCC), United States [M]
College Theology Society (CTS)

Committee for Incorporation of Women's Perspectives into Curriculum (CIWPC) [M]

Communitas, Washington, DC [F]

Communities of the Christian Spirit, Blue Bell and Noble, PA [D,F]

Communities of Peace and Friendship [M]

Community of the Anawim, Denver, CO [E]

Companions of Chiara - Vestments for Women [C]

Conference for Catholic Lesbians (CCL), New York, NY [A,E,F,I,J,M]

Consultants, Annapolis, MD

Corps of Retired Priests United for Service, Morris, NJ [A,C,F,I,J,K,M,N]

CORPUS, Morris, NJ [A,C,F,I,J,K,M,N]

Creation-Centered Catholic Communities (CCCC), St. Louis, MO [M]

CREDO Liturgical Dance Company of Boston [D]

Cross Cultural Christian Concerns (CCCC), Oak Park, IL [F]

Dignity/USA [A,B,E,H,I,J,K,N]

Domestic Catholic Church [F]

Droits et Libertes dans Les Eglises (France) [N]

Dromenon Center for Sacred Psychology, Boca Raton, FL [F]

Ecumenical Feminist Roundtable [D]

Eighth Day Center for Justice, Chicago, IL [E,F,M]

Eighth of May (Netherlands)

Emmaus Communities [B,F]

Esther House Groups [F]

European Conference for Human Rights in the Church [N]

European Network

Family Life Ministry, Rockaway Park, NY and Brooklyn, NY [F]

Federation of Christian Ministries (FCM), Upper Darby, PA [F,I,K,N]

Fellowship of Southern Illinois Laity (FOSIL), Belleville, IL [A,B,F,J]

Feminism and Faith, Indianapolis, IN [D]

Feminist Action Coalition, Jersey City, NJ [E]

Feminist Liturgy Group [D]

Freelance Faith Group, Chicago, IL [F]

Friends of Creation Spirituality, Oakland, CA[F,I,M]

Friends of the Third World, Fort Wayne, IN [B,F]

Future of the American Church Conference [M]

FutureChurch [A,B,I,J]

Gathering for Rituals of Women (GROW) [D]

GOD'S CHILD Project, Bismarck, ND [F]

Good Tidings, Canadansis, PA [F]

Grail, Grailville and Grailville Conference [M]

Grail Women Task Force, Loveland, OH [E]

Green Nation, San Jose, CA [B,F]

Greenhouse Experiment, Greer, SC [F]

Groundwork for a Just World, Detroit, MI [F]
Group, The, Vacaville, CA [F]
HELIX, Silver Spring, MD [D]
House-Church [F]
Immaculate Heart Community, Los Angeles [B]
Institute for Culture and Creation Spirituality (ICCS) [M]
Institute of the Blessed Virgin, Wheaton, IL [B]
Institute of Women Today (IWT), Chicago, IL [E,M]
International Thomas Merton Society [F]
Island Ecospirituality Centre, (Prince Edward Island) [B,F]
James Markunas Society, San Francisco, CA [F]
Justice Campaign [M]
Kairos Community, Rochester, NY [F]
Keryx, Morris Plains, NJ [F]
Kirche von Unten (Germany)
Koinonia Community, Lake Oswego, OR [F]
Latin American North American Church Concerns, Notre Dame, IN [F]
Lay Conference of Women Religious (LCWR)
Leadership Conference of Women Religious (LCWR) [M]
Let Live [M]
Life and Light Ministries, Houston, TX [F]
Limina [M]
Listen to the Voices of the People [M]
Looking Toward the Light, Natuck, MA [F]
Loretto Women's Network, St. Louis, MO [E,F,G,H,I,M]
Love Happens, Monte Clare, PA [F]
Magdalene Group, Oshkosh, WI [F]
Mary's Pence [B,F,M]
Matrix, Oshkosh, WI [F]
Mercy Justice Coalition Committee, Omaha, NE [E]
Miriam's Circle, Waldwick, NJ [F]
Miryam Community, Highland Park, IL [D]
Moveable Feasts [D]
Movement for the Ordination of Married Men (MOMM), (Great
    Britain)
National Assembly of Religious Women (NARW), Chicago, IL [M]
National Association for a Married Priesthood (CORPUS),
    Morris, NJ [A,C,F,I,J,K,M,N]
National Association for Lay Ministry [H,M]
National Association for Pastoral Renewal (NAPR)
National Association of Catholic Diocesan Lesbian
    and Gay Ministries [H]

National Association of Parish Coordinators and Directors
  of Religious Education [H]
National Black Sister's Conference (NBSC), Washington, DC [F]
National Catholic Education Association (NCEA) [H,M]
National Center for Evangelization and Parish Renewal (NCEPR)
National Center for Pastoral Leadership (NCPL, formerly Time)
National Coalition of American Nuns (NCAN), Chicago, IL [E,F,G,H,I,M]
National Federation of Priest's Councils [H]
NETWORK: A National Catholic Social Justice Lobby [B,H,M]
New Jerusalem Community, Cincinnati, OH [F]
New Visions, Mount Prospect, IL [F]
New Ways Ministry, Mt. Ranier, MD [E,F,I,K,M,N]
NEWoman, Luxemburg, WI [F]
North American Conference of Separated and Divorced Catholics [M]
Nova Community Women's Groups [D]
Ocean of Glory, Crofton, MD [D]
Oecoumin, Walton, IL [F]
Open Window, Dallas, TX [B,F]
Pallottine Apostolic Association, Milwaukee, WI [F]
Pandora's Circle, Tuxedo, NY [F]
Parish Renewal Consulting Services (PRCS), San Francisco, CA [F,I,J]
Pathfinder Renewal Weekend, Palm Desert, CA [F]
Pax Christi USA, Erie, PA [F,H,I,K,N]
People of the Promise [F]
Performing Arts Ministry (PAM)
Prayerfulness Support Group (PSG), Bastrop, TX [B,F]
Priests and People for a Married Priesthood (PPMP), Minneapolis, MN
Priests for Equality [F,K]
Project Search, Inc., Burbank, IL [F]
Promises, Alexandria, VA and Englewood, CO [F]
Quest and Vision Study Groups [F]
Quixote Center [Convergence Task Force], Hyattsville, MD [E,K,M,N]
Renewal Coordinating Community, Garden City, NY [A,B,F,I,N]
Rent-A-Priest [M]
Response-Ability, Rosemont, PA [F]
Roncalli Connection, Sterling, IL [F]
Roncalli Society, Bloomington, IL [F]
Ruah, Holyoke, MA [D]
Sarah's Circle, Midland, MI and Binghamton, NY [D,F]
Sarah's Sisters [D]
Sea of Faith Network, San Francisco, CA [F]
Shalom Center, Splendora, TX [F]
SHEM Center for Interfaith Spirituality, Oak Park, IL [F]

Sinsinawa Network on Women's Issues, Atlanta, GA [E]
Sisters Against Sexism (SAS) [D]
Sisters for Christian Community, Freehold, NJ [F]
Sisters in Solidarity (SIS) [D]
Sisters, Servants of the Immaculate Heart of Mary, Monroe, MI [B]
Small Faith Communities (SFCs) [F]
Solinox, Reston, VA [D]
Sophia House [D,F]
Spirit, Columbus, OH [D]
Spiritual Directions, South Euclid, OH [F]
Spirituality of the Feminine in Action (SOFIA) [F]
St. Benedict's Educational Centre, Winnipeg [B]
SteppingStone, Milwaukee, WI [F]
Student Advocates for Inclusive Ministry (SAIM), Notre Dame, IN [F]
Table Talk, Libertyville, IL [F]
TAU Volunteers, Chicago, IL [F]
Thomas Merton Center, Palo Alto, CA [B,F]
Time Consultants, Annapolis, MD
United States Catholic Biblical Association (USCBA)
Upper Room Community, The Woodlands, TX [F]
Voices of Catholic Action (VOCA), Altadena, CA [F]
Volunteer Missionary Movement, Greendale, WI [F]
Vroumens (Netherlands)
Weavers of Change, Grand Junction, CO [F]
Wellstreams Center, Chicago, IL [F]
WIT, Lincoln, NE [D]
Womanchurch or Womenchurch [Convergence] [E,J]
Womanspirit [D]
Women at the Well, San Jose, CA [F]
WoMen Gathering, Lacon, IL [F]
Women's Alliance for Theology, Ethics and Ritual (WATER) [E,F,G]
Women's Eucharist Groups [F]
Women's Institute on Religion and Society [D]
Women's Interfaith Meditation Circle, Toronto [D]
Women's Liturgy Group, West Palm Beach, FL [F]
Women's Option, The (TWO), Dayton, OH [D]
Women's Ordination Conference (WOC) [A,E,F,I,J,K,N]
Women's Spirituality Groups [D,F]
Women's Worship (Circle) [D,F]
Womenprayer [D]
Woodlands, The, Osseo, WI [F]
Worship and Equality, Belfast, North Ireland [B,F]
Young Feminist Network (YFN, a project of WOC)

^A Members of Catholic Organizations for Renewal (COR).

^B Organizations cosponsoring the 1996 Detroit CTA Conference.

^C Organizations with exhibits at the 1996 Detroit CTA Conference.

^D Resource organizations listed in Diann L. Neu and Mary E. Hunt, "Women-Church Sourcebook." Women's Alliance for Theology, Ethics and Ritual (WATER), WATERworks Press, 1993, appendix entitled "Women-Church Directory."

^E Women-Church Convergence Member Organizations, as listed in Diann L. Neu and Mary E. Hunt, "Women-Church Sourcebook." Women's Alliance for Theology, Ethics and Ritual (WATER), WATERworks Press, 1993, appendix entitled "Women-Church Directory."

^F Organizations listed in Call to Action. "Renewing Our Church: 307 Small Faith Communities and Church Renewal Organizations," 1997 Edition.

^G Signers of a full-page ad supporting Medicaid funding of abortion. This ad was placed in *Roll Call* (Capitol Hill's twice-weekly newspaper for Congressmen and their staffs). *The Wanderer*, November 4, 1993.

^H Endorsers of the 4th National Symposium on "A National Dialogue on Lesbian/Gay Issues and Catholicism," sponsored by New Ways Ministry, Pittsburgh, Pennsylvania, March 7-9, 1997.

^I Member organizations of Catholic Organizations for Renewal (COR).

^J Organizations cooperating with the Parish Renewal Consulting Service (PRCS) project, as listed in "We Are Church: Reflections on Core Values and Concerns." PRCS, 1996, inside front cover.

^K Members of the We Are Church Coalition.

^L Bernard Cardinal Law. "A Theological Wasteland." *The Pilot*, June 20, 1997.

^M More detailed information on these organizations can be found in Donna Steichen's book *Ungodly Rage: The Hidden Face of Catholic Feminism*. San Francisco: Ignatius Press, 1992.

^N These organizations have formally endorsed the "Charter of the Rights of Catholics in the Church," written by the Association for the Rights of Catholic in the Church (ARCC).

ENDNOTES

1 Anthony Padovano, President of CORPUS, the National Society for a Married Priesthood, "From Cathedral to Cafeteria Catholic: An Exploration of Personal Conscience and Catholic Identity." Talk given at the Call to Action National Convention in Detroit's Cobo Hall, November 15-17, 1996.

2 Frank Bonnike, co-founder of CORPUS, quoted in Cheryl L. Tan. "Priests from CORPUS: Catholics are Bending the Rules to Fill the Gaps Left Behind the Altar." *CORPUS Reports*, November-December 1995, page 5.

3 Father John Courtney Murray, S.J., principle author of Vatican II's *Declaration on Religious Freedom*, quoted in Russell Shaw. "Answers." *National Catholic Register*, September 13, 1992, page 4.

4 Kathleen Howley. "Strange Sisters." *The Catholic World Report*, January 1996, pages 30 to 32.

5 Undated CITI News release entitled "21 Catholic Church Laws Validate Married Priests."

6 For further exposition on dissent and obedience, see *Lumen Gentium* ("Dogmatic Constitution on the Church"), November 21, 1964, #12, 22.

7 Mary Grace Crowley-Kock, CORPUS Midwest regional coordinator, quoted in Cheryl L. Tan. "Priests from CORPUS: Catholics are Bending the Rules to Fill the Gaps Left Behind the Altar." *CORPUS Reports*, November-December 1995, page 5.

8 Ralph and Linda Pinto of CORPUS. "Back to the Future." Talk given at the Call to Action National Convention in Detroit's Cobo Hall, November 15-17, 1996.

9 "A New Vision of Catholic Social Justice." *Equal Is as Equal Does: Challenging Vatican Views on Women.* Women-Church Convergence, 1995. Also quoted in *We Are Church: Reflections on Core Values and Concerns.* Parish Renewal Consulting Services (PRCS), 1996, page 15.

10 Rosemary Radford Ruether. "Why I Stay in the Church." *Sojourners*, July 1994, pages 15 to 17.

11 Dianne Neu and Mary E. Hunt. "Women of Fire: A Pentecost Event." Washington, D.C.: Women's Alliance for Theology, Ethics and Ritual (WATER), 1990, page 9.

12 As described in Msgr. William Smith, *"Humanae Vitae*, Dissent, and Infallibility," a presentation at Human Life International's World Conference on Love, Life, and the Family, held in Santa Clara, California in March, 1991. St. Vincent of Lerins stated, "Moreover, in the Catholic Church itself, all possible care must be taken, that we hold that faith which has been believed everywhere, always, by all. For that is truly and in the strictest sense 'Catholic,' which, as the name itself and the reason of the thing declare, comprehends all universally. This rule we shall observe if we follow universality, antiquity, consent. We shall follow universality if we confess that one faith to be true, which the whole Church throughout the world confesses; antiquity, if we in no wise depart from those interpretations which it is manifest were notoriously held by our holy ancestors and fathers; consent, in like manner, if in antiquity itself we adhere to the consistent definitions and determinations of all, or at the least of almost all priests and doctors." (*The Commonitory* of St. Vincent of Lerins, Chapter II [6], "A General Rule for Distinguishing the Truth of the Catholic Faith from the Falsehood of Heretical Pravity," 434 A.D.).

13 Anthony T. Padovano. "Power, Sex and Church Structures." Undated CORPUS Research Paper Number Four, pages 5 and 7. Many of the claims in this paper are repeated in different words in "A History of Celibacy in the Catholic Church," an undated Call to Action/FutureChurch brochure.

14 Example Scriptures on **adultery**: Exodus 20:14; Leviticus 18:20, 19:20, 20:10-12; Deuteronomy 5:18, 22:22, 27:20; Proverbs 6:25-32; Matthew 5:27-32, 15:19, 19:9, 19:18; Mark 7:21, 10:11-12, 10:19; Luke 16:18, 18:20; John 8:11; Romans 7:3, 13:9; Colossians 6:9; Galatians 5:19. **Fornication**: Exodus 22:16-17; Leviticus 19:29; Deuteronomy 22:14-24; Matthew 15:19,19:9; Mark 7:21;10:11; 1 Corinthians 5:11,6:9,6:13,6:18; Galatians 5:19; Ephesians 5:3, 5:5. **Divorce**: Matthew 19:6-9,; Mark 10:11-12; Luke 16:18. **Sodomy and homosexuality**: Genesis 13:13, 19:1-29; Leviticus 18:22, 20:13; Deuteronomy 23:17,22-25; 29:23; 32:32; Judges 19:20-26; 1 Kings 14:24; 15:12; 22:46; 2 Kings 23:7; 1 Timothy 1:9-10; Wisdom 14:26-27; Ezekiel 16:46,48,49; Luke 17:29; Romans 1:22, 26-32; 1 Corinthians 6:9,10; Jude 7.

15 St. Augustine, *De Moribus Manichaeorum*, Chapter 17, #63.

16 Rosemary Radford Ruether. "Radical Victorians: The Quest for an Alternative Culture." *Women and Religion in America*. Volume 3, 1900-1968. San Francisco: Harper and Row, 1986, pages xiv and 3.

[17] As described in Donna Steichen. "Women-Church Synod in Cincinnati." *Fidelity* Magazine, December 1987, pages 21 to 31.

[18] Dianne L. Neu and Mary E. Hunt. "Women-Church Sourcebook." Women's Alliance for Theology, Ethics and Ritual (WATER), Washington, D.C., 1993.

[19] "Lucy's Cards and Posters," catalog distributed at a booth at the 1996 Call to Action conference, page 4.

[20] Undated Young Feminist Network flyer entitled "Why a Young Feminist Network?"

[21] Mary Daly, quoted in "Anger with the Church." Undated Women's Ordination Conference pullout section entitled "New Woman, New Church."

[22] Cf. 1 Kings 21:40 and Jeremiah 19:5, 32:35.

[23] Bernard Cooke, in his talk at the 1995 national Call to Action conference, quoted in "Inside Call to Action." *Crisis* Magazine, February 1996.

[24] As described in Mary Meehan. "How Can They Be Called Catholic?" *National Catholic Register*, November 19, 1989, page 5.

[25] Christine Schenk, CSJ. "The Future of Priestly Ministry." Talk given at the Call to Action National Conference in Detroit's Cobo Hall, November 15-17, 1996.

[26] Sister Maureen Fiedler, quoted in Kieron Wood. "Boring From Within." *Catholic World Report*, December 1995, page 21.

[27] Daniel A. Helminiak. "Catholicism, Homosexuality and Dignity: Questions and Answers about Being Lesbian, Gay, Bisexual or Transgendered and Catholic." Dignity/USA brochure, 1996. Also in *We Are Church: Reflections on Core Values and Concerns.* Parish Renewal Consulting Services (PRCS), 1996, pages 35 to 37.

[28] Christine Schenk, CSJ, quoted in William Simbro. "Nun Calls Priest Shortage Artificial." *The Des Moines Register*, February 13, 1997, page 2M.

[29] Elizabeth A. Johnson. "Women's Ordination and Responsible Dissent." *We Are Church: Reflections on Core Values and Concerns.* Parish Renewal Consulting Services (PRCS), 1996, page 20.

[30] Sister Theresa Kane. "A New Millennium: Women Breaking through a Patriarchal Church." Talk given at the Call to Action National Convention in Detroit's Cobo Hall, November 15-17, 1996.

[31] Rosemary Radford Ruether. *Womanguides: Readings Toward a Feminist Theology.* Beacon Press, 1985, page 104.

32   Dignity/USA brochure entitled "Catholicism, Homosexuality and Dignity: Questions & Answers about Being Lesbian, Gay, Bisexual or Transgendered and Catholic, 1996"; and Rosemary Radford Ruether. "Goddesses and Witches: Liberation and Counter-Cultural Feminism." *Christian Century*, September 10-17, 1980, page 842.

33   These calculations were made in a LOTUS 123 spreadsheet with figures from P.J. Kenedy & Sons' *Official Catholic Directories*, 1956 to 1997 Editions, and the Vatican Secretary of State *Statistical Yearbook of the Church*, 1975, 1981, 1987 and 1993 annuals. This spreadsheet is available from Brian Clowes, Human Life International, 4 Family Life, Front Royal, Virginia 22630, on a 3.5" high-density disk for $5, which is the cost of duplicating, shipping and handling the disk. The spreadsheet shows the number of priests, religious sisters, ordinations and Catholics by diocese for each of the past 40 years, and the calculations supporting the numerical conclusions of this booklet. For the purposes of this study, the term "orthodox" means a diocese that has exhibited a general predisposition towards fidelity towards the Magisterium since Vatican II. Naturally, every diocese has experienced instances of infiltration and activism by those who disagree with or dissent from Catholic teaching and, at times, suffer from a perception by orthodox lay people of inaction on the part of their bishops. The following 15 dioceses have followed a generally orthodox tradition since Vatican II: Amarillo, Texas; Arlington, Virginia; Atlanta, Georgia; Baltimore, Maryland; Corpus Christi, Texas; Denver, Colorado; Fargo, North Dakota; Fort Wayne-South Bend, Indiana; Lincoln and Omaha, Nebraska; Peoria, Illinois; Philadelphia, Pennsylvania; Sioux Falls, South Dakota; Steubenville, Ohio; and Wichita, Kansas. For the purposes of this study, the term "progressive" means a diocese that has exhibited a general predisposition towards liberal activism and systematic toleration towards dissent from the Magisterium since Vatican II. Of course, all dioceses, no matter how liberal, have occasionally or even systematically displayed orthodoxy in certain areas. The following 15 dioceses have followed a generally progressive tradition since Vatican II: Chicago, Illinois; Detroit and Grand Rapids, Michigan; Los Angeles, California; Madison and Milwaukee, Wisconsin; New Ulm, Minnesota; Phoenix, Arizona; Portland, Maine; Rockville Centre, New York; San Bernardino, San Diego and San Francisco, California; Seattle, Washington; and Tucson, Arizona. The terms "orthodox" and "progressive" are necessarily subjective, and 15 dioceses of each persuasion were selected after an extensive review of

articles carried in four publications over the past 30 years: *National Catholic Reporter, National Catholic Register, Commonweal* and *The Wanderer.* A list of these dioceses were then submitted to a number of individuals with extensive knowledge of the history of the American Catholic Church for confirmation and correction.

[34] Richard Schoenherr. *Full Pews and Empty Altars.* Also quoted in Louise Haggett, "Need a Priest? Ask a Married Catholic Priest!" *We Are Church: Reflections on Core Values and Concerns.* Parish Renewal Consulting Services (PRCS), 1996, page 25. This claim is repeated in an undated "Promises" flyer, 1559 Rockville Pike, Box 99, Rockville, MD 26902.

[35] CORPUS. "ANNOUNCING: Top Ten Reasons Why the Pope Should Allow a Married Priesthood." This material is contained in a flyer by the same name and in *We Are Church: Reflections on Core Values and Concerns.* Parish Renewal Consulting Services (PRCS), 1996, page 27.

[36] Bill Callahan. "Building a Democratic Church: A More Vibrant Way to Follow Jesus." *Churchwatch*, February/March 1995, page 4.

[37] FutureChurch and Call to Action. Undated flyer entitled "The Priest Shortage at a Glance."

[38] "Worldwide Parishes without Resident Pastors." *CARA Report*, Spring 1997, page 5. Center for Applied Research in the Apostolate, Georgetown University.

[39] Donna Amy Podobinski. "Servants of Christ's Priesthood: Revitalizing God's People." Framingham, MA: Celibacy Is The Issue (CITI), 1995, page 15.

[40] Robert Barzan. "Leaving the Priesthood: Practical Advice for Roman Catholic Priests and Religious Men." San Francisco: White Crane Press, 1996, page 9.

[41] Marianne Duddy. "Gay-Lesbian Issues in Today's Church." Talk given at the Call to Action National Convention in Detroit's Cobo Hall, November 15-17, 1996.

[42] 1980 membership figures are from Bernard Quinn, *et.al. Churches and Church Membership in the United States, 1980.* Atlanta, Georgia: Glenmary Research Center, 1982. Table 1, "Churches and Church Membership by denomination, for the U.S.: 1980," pages 1 to 3. 1992 figures are from United States Department of Commerce, Bureau of the Census. Reference Book and Guide to Sources, *Statistical Abstract of the United States*, 1995 (115th Edition). Table 84: "Religious Bodies—Selected Data." 1997 figures are exponentially extrapolated using the average growth rates experienced by each denomination during the period 1980 to

1992. The Assembly of God, Fundamentalist, Islam, Jehovah's Witnesses, Lutheran Church (Missouri Synod), Mormon, and Southern Baptist denominations have increased their memberships from 31,108,000 in 1982 to 40,379,367 in 1997, an increase of 29.8 percent. The Disciples of Christ, Episcopalian, Presbyterian (USA), United Church of Christ, and United Methodist denominations have seen their combined memberships decrease from 21,140,000 in 1982 to 16,073,868 in 1997, a loss of 24.0 percent during this period.

43 "CARA Examines Vocation Trends of Members of Religious Communities." *CARA Report*, Winter 1997, pages 1 and 6. Center for Applied Research in the Apostolate, Georgetown University.

44 Anne Stewart Connell. "*Sisters in Crisis*—Reviews." *Religious Life* (Institute on Religious Life), July-August 1997, pages 8 and 12.

45 Joseph Cardinal Ratzinger, quoted in Avery Dulles, S.J. "Travails of Dialogue." *Crisis*, February 1997, pages 16 to 20.

46 Fran Ferder, FSPA and Rev. John Heagle. "Faithfulness to the Gospel: Key to Ongoing Renewal," Talk given at the Call to Action National Conference in Detroit's Cobo Hall, November 15-17, 1996.

47 Bernard Cardinal Law of Boston, quoted in David Scott. "A Search for Common Ground in a 'Time of Peril.'" *Our Sunday Visitor*, August 25, 1996.

48 Father Art Baranowski, *Call to Action News*, December 1995-January 1996.

49 Rosemary Bleuher, Virginia Hoffman, Professor at Loyola University in Chicago, and Father Ron Purenowski of Detroit. Panel talk entitled "Drawing on our Collective Wisdom," given at the Call to Action National Convention in Detroit's Cobo Hall, November 15-17, 1996.

50 Bishop Albert Ottenweller and Nancy Westmeyer, OSF. "Patriarchy to Partnership." Talk given at the Call to Action National Convention in Detroit's Cobo Hall, November 15-17, 1996.

51 "Bishop Continues Silence on Protestors." Call to Action Northern Virginia newsletter, April 1995, page 1.

52 Louise Haggett, Founder of Celibacy Is The Issue (CITI), quoted in Cheryl L. Tan. "Priests from CORPUS: Catholics are Bending the Rules to Fills the Gaps Left Behind the Altar." *CORPUS Reports*, November-December 1995, page 3.

53 As described in Robert P. Lockwood. "Catholic Journal: Some Things Just Speak for Themselves." *Our Sunday Visitor*, 1997.

54 Edmund Burke. *Thoughts on the Cause of the Present Discontents*, April 23, 1770.

55 Brian Clowes. *The Facts of Life*. Front Royal, Virginia: Human Life International, 1997, page 318. The number of surgical abortions is updated to the end of 1997. According to the 1997 *Official Catholic Directory*, there were 9 cardinals, 408 archbishops and bishops, 48,097 priests, 87,644 sisters, 11,788 permanent deacons, and 6,293 religious brothers in the United States as of December 31, 1996. There were also 61,207,914 Catholics out of a total U.S. population of 268,299,833, so 22.81 percent of the U.S. population is Catholic. This ratio was applied to the total number of abortions (37.9 million) to arrive at an approximation of the number of legal surgical abortions committed by Catholic women since 1966 (8.6 million), or 14.1 percent of the current Catholic population. This ratio is then applied to the current number of men and women religious to arrive at the number of future religious who have been aborted.

56 California, Colorado and North Carolina legalized abortion in 1967; Georgia and Maryland in 1968; Arkansas, Delaware, Kansas, New Mexico, and Oregon in 1969; and Hawaii, Alaska, New York, and Washington in 1970. The time period during which this drop in baptisms took place was three years before surgical abortion legalization to three years after surgical abortion legalization.

57 Father Thomas L. Kinkead. *An Explanation of the Baltimore Catechism* (also known as the *Baltimore Catechism No. 4*), Questions 122 through 127.

INDEX

Miceli, Father Vincent P., 92
Murray, Father John Courtney, 8
National Catholic Register, 90
National Catholic Reporter, 94
National Coalition of American Nuns (NCAN), 52
National Security Study Memo (NSSM) 200, 54
Natural law, 47
Neu, Dianne, 37, 39, 80
Neumann Press, 91
New Oxford Review, 90
Oddie, Father William, 92
Our Blessed Lady of Victory Mission, 91
Our Lady's Book Service, 91
Padovano, Anthony, 8, 23, 27
Paganism
    Pagan liturgies, 44
Parish Renewal Consulting Services (PRCS), 51
Pascendi Dominici Gregis (1907), 7, 24, 25, 29, 30, 35, 36, 46, 75, 77
Pax Christi, 94
Pinto, Ralph and Linda, 19, 57
Pope Joan II, 105
Pope Pius XII, 50
Pride, 36
"Priest shortage," 54
Ratzinger, Joseph Cardinal
    On dialogue, 70
RENEW Program, 73
Roman Catholic Books, 91
Roman Catholic Faithful, Inc. (RCF), 86, 93
Ruether, Rosemary Radford, 20, 31, 52
    Claim that 9,000,000 women were burned for witchcraft, 53
St. Augustine, 28
St. Joseph Foundation, 86
Schenk, Christine, 44, 50
Sin
    Redefining the concept of "sin," 47
Small faith communities (SFCs), 71
Sophia, 32-33
Sophia Institute Press, 91
"Star Trek," 19-20
Steichen, Donna, 92
Sun Tzu, 1
Sursum Corda!, 90